From Top Mountain

From Top Mountain

AN AUTOBIOGRAPHY

Bishop Dr Joe Aldred

First published in 2015
by Hansib Publications Limited
P.O. Box 226, Hertford, Hertfordshire
SG14 3WY, United Kingdom

info@hansibpublications.com
www.hansibpublications.com

ISBN 978-1-910553-20-6

A CIP catalogue record for this book
is available from the British Library

Production
Hansib Publications Limited

Printed in Great Britain

Dedication

This book is dedicated to all the people who have contributed to making my life what it is. I thank God for: my parents Jonathan and Iona Aldred; my ten siblings James, Lester, Hosea, Paul, Timothy, Cynthia, Gloria, Ruth, Jeremiah and Winsome; my wife and No. 1 supporter Novelette, our three daughters Marsha, Genelle and Alethea; son in law Andrew; our grandchildren Krystal, Arooj, Luke and Ellis. To the mothers and fathers in the faith who pray for me and support me; my friends, too many to mention, whose companionship has been invaluable. To my professional colleagues who challenge and sharpen me, and to my critics who challenge and sharpen me even more. To those who have been there at critical junctions in my life, some of whom are mentioned in the book. To everyone who has impacted my life in any way, thank you.

Contents

Preface

Over the past twenty years I have made a determined effort to broadcast, write and publish. I do this because of my belief that it is important to tell your own story, or others will tell it for you from their perspective. Having one's story published in a book is a way of bringing it to a wider audience and preserving it for future generations. This is my story, told by me. Those who have shared some of these moments and experiences may have different recollections to mine, but these are my recollections. I have tried to be as generous as possible.

I hope you enjoy reading my musings of a life that started in Jamaica and has been lived in England for over forty five years now. It has been an interesting ride and I thank God that I have been able to make a small contribution to our common humanity. I have divided the book into the natural sections of my life beginning with my time in Jamaica and in England since 1968 when I arrived as a fifteen year old.

CHAPTER 1

From Top Mountain to Smethwick 1952-1968

Top Mountain is a rural district in St Catherine, Jamaica. It is located next to a sister district called Paul Mountain. At the time of my birth in 1952, neither districts had any industry; the people lived off naturally fertile lands. The small communities had no gas, electricity or running water. Those wanting to improve their life chances moved to Kingston or migrated abroad.

I was born in Top Mountain, the eighth of eleven children to Iona Caroline and Jonathan John Aldred. Allow me to introduce you to my siblings in descending order: James, Lester, Hosea, Paul, Timothy, Cynthia, Gloria, (me), Ruth, Jeremiah (Jerry) and Winsome. It remains a marvel to me that a diminutive woman like our mother could produce so many children. In that era, my family was not exceptional in this regard. What may be exceptional about us though is that our mother had the first of us, my eldest brother James, before she had reached her fifteenth birthday. Somehow mum and dad, Saana and Bra John, as we call them, stayed together after their inauspicious start. And I for one am eternally grateful for their dedication to each other and to their children.

Of my wider family, I know little though I have thought often about delving into my ancestry. Two of my grandparents died before I was born; so I knew only a grandmother from my father's side and a grandfather from my mother's side, and he I met only once. My father's mother, Sister Mammy, I spend lots of time with. She had lost use of a hand as a baby when she fell into a fire. She was a great example of how to make the most of what you have. There seemed to be nothing a fully able-bodied person could do that Sister Mammy could not do. She died when I was still quite young.

Of other family, I knew only a sister of my dad's and some cousins. Growing up in Jamaica, my siblings formed the core and almost the entirety of family.

My pet name was Cutty, although I do not recall being called it much. I suspect it was a name used by my older siblings who left home before I, at number eight, had gained much traction and the tradition never got passed down to my younger siblings. Almost everybody I knew growing up had a pet name to accompany their proper name. There would invariably be a cause for the pet name. Cutty was based on my early display of dislike for sharing my food. One imagines that in a large family sharing was a necessity. But I am told that to ask to cut a piece off my flour dumpling or yam was to court my strong displeasure. Maybe 'Don't cut it' was a more appropriate pet name.

Top Mountain can best be described as a deep rural area. Most of its inhabitants were poor. We lived in a tiny two-room bungalow and to this day, I wonder how as large a family as ours managed in such a small house. Fortunately the thirteen of us, Saana, Bra John and eleven children, never lived together at the same time. In fact, the eleven siblings have never been in one place at one time!

I have sometimes jokingly said I grew up in a detached house: the bedrooms were detached from the bathroom, which was detached from the kitchen which was detached from the toilet, which itself was detached from the mango tree stump at the front of our yard that acted as a dining table. Everything apart from the concrete block built twin rooms were made of insubstantial material and were short distance walks from where we slept in the twin rooms.

Water had to be captured from rainfall or fetched from a standpipe a mile away - when it was available. Cooking was always on an open fire with logs. Lighting was by kerosene lamps or lantern, but at times, we resorted to crude bottle lamps by lighting the cork of a bottle containing kerosene oil. We were poor.

And yet the quarter acre of land on which we lived was fertile and rich with cultivation. Our mum, Saana, could often be seen planting seeds and seedlings of one sort or another, from yam and cassava to gonga peas, to red peas, from pumpkin seeds to melon seeds. You name it, Saana planted it. Anything that would bear fruit to feed the family, she planted.

Growing up with Saana and some siblings I learned to dig yam, cocoa and cassava mounds, or hills as we called them. I helped to cultivate sweet and Irish potatoes, chocho, dashine, runner beans and more. Saana taught us by example to manage the soil to feed ourselves.

All around us were fruit trees of various sorts: mangoes, jackfruit, coconuts, cashew nuts, naesberry, sweet sop, sour sop, coffee, bananas, and more. Our family plot provided food all year round.

In addition to the family plot there were two other pieces of land our family owned: one we called 'Outa Road' and one 'Uppa Wood'. Outa Road was probably an acre in the adjoining district of Paul Mountain and was bequeathed to us by the woman who brought up our dad. Uppa Wood was further away, and less developed than either the family plot or Outa Road. Both supplied vegetation though they did not have the daily tending of mum's green fingers as did the family plot.

Outa Road certainly had the best 'Number Eleven' mango tree anywhere on the planet and during mango season, it was a pleasure to stand under it and risk being hit on the head by a falling ripe Number Eleven mango. Uppa Wood had many mango trees and it is from there that during mango seasons we would fetch donkey hamper loads of mangoes for Spanish Town market. Uppa Wood, as its name suggest, had lots of log wood that my second eldest brother, Lester, would regularly use to make 'coalskill' that produced man made coal to sell to better off people who bought it at the Spanish Town market as fuel for cooking fires or to heat up clothes irons. It is Uppa Wood too that holds one of my most gruesome childhood memories.

We had a family donkey called Prince. Like the other animals we kept for sale or domestic use such as chickens, cows, goats and pigs, Prince had to be kept in places where it could graze. This meant moving it regularly to new grazing plots. The chickens and pigs were kept at home, but Uppa Wood, though far from home (as a child I imagined it was ten miles away, but I realise now it is probably three to four miles) provided excellent feeding ground for animals.

One of the cardinal rules was that the animals should not be tethered on a hillside but always on a level. Another rule was they must be relocated each day, if possible, and certainly every other day. We tended to move them to new grazing areas every other day when they grazed Uppa Wood. But this meant walking the three to four miles there and back each time.

On one infamous occasion, Saana woke me up early in the morning to go Uppa Wood to move Prince to a new feeding spot. This was the every other day. I left home, walked a mile or so and decided I just could not make it to Uppa Wood that day! I dilly dallied for about the time I might be expected to take and returned home giving the impression I had been and had done my duty to Prince by moving him to a new grazing area. I had not.

This meant that by the time I went to Uppa Wood, poor Prince had been in the same spot for four days; and I had tethered him on a hillside. Prince had seemingly become agitated, walked repeatedly around the tree to which he was tied, became entangled with nearby trees until the rope around his neck had become taught and strangled him. Prince, the family donkey, was dead. I had killed the family donkey and Saana was not pleased! It was some considerable time afterwards, like years, before I admitted what had actually happened and since then I have never lived down being responsible for killing the family donkey.

I learned Machiavellian ways quite early in life. It is always doing your best and never exposing your frailties. Seeing how mongooses preyed on chicks and how hawks swooped surreptitiously to pierce their victims and flew away with them taught me almost by osmosis how to get the best out of situations. I learned how to pick young unripe fruits and hide them buried for ripening, but hidden from animals and birds that would devour them. There was at least one occasion when things backfired. Badly. Saana sent me on an errand to plant some gonga peas at Uppa Wood. I went, but planting gonga peas was arduous business. After carefully planting a few holes with approximately six peas in each, I looked up and saw the expanse I still had to cover. I decided to hurry things up by planting handfuls in each hole. Well, my planting chore was over in little time. Problem was, a couple of weeks later when several pea shoots emerged jostling for space above the ground, it was plain for all to see what I had done! Saana smiled knowingly.

My dad, Bra John, migrated to England in 1955 when I was two years old. He was part of the economic migratory pattern prevalent, post-World War 2, that saw people being pushed and pulled towards the United States, England, Canada and elsewhere in the Caribbean. I will return to the relationship between my father and me later. Suffice it to say now that although he returned briefly to Jamaica in 1959, I did not grow up with him being around, and I am the product of a single parent upbringing until a month before my sixteenth birthday. But it was not mum alone who brought me up. I am the product of the imbibed African philosophy that 'it takes a village to raise a child'.

My older siblings helped in my childhood rearing, our neighbours helped, church elders helped, as did teachers at school. I grew up as a real country bumpkin, but within an incredibly supportive and creative space that shaped my character for life.

As an eighth child in a family where dad was five thousand miles away, with two sisters immediately my seniors and another immediately my junior; being sandwiched between matriarchies has been character forming. How interesting that having married I find myself with three daughters and wife for company!

When mum was away, my two elder sisters took it upon themselves to be head of the family - at least head over me! This was especially so after our brother above both sisters had left home. And where mother would not resort to corporal punishment, my sisters sometimes would. I decided that violence was the answer to the violence they perpetrated on me, and I threatened my eldest sister with a macka stick. If the reader does not know what a 'macka stick' is then just take my word for it that it is pretty sharp! That threat seemed to do the trick, and from that day, I do not recall her ever threatening to beat me again. These same sisters who took delight in keeping me under 'heavy manners' at home were quick to defend me their little brother at school. And we are best of siblings now of course.

As I got older, one of my elder brothers, Paul, who no longer lived at home, thought he would make use of me as cook whilst he and others worked the fields. So I would invariably be taken with him and other work colleagues to the fields where they worked digging yam and cassava hills, mostly on Saturdays.

One day, as I cooked a big spider fell into the pot, which was always open when cooking because it had no lid. It was immediately cooked through and I carefully removed this dismembered multi legged spider from the pot leaving no trace when the food was shared between the men at lunchtime. Knowing what I knew, however, I decided I would not partake of the meal I had cooked. Somehow, I seemed to escape suspicion.

The same brother got a job at a cane plantation at Innswood in St Catherine, and often asked me to make fried dumplings for his lunch. To do this meant waking up very early, probably around 4am since he needed to be at work for five or six o'clock! I didn't much like getting up that early.

On one occasion as I was making the dough in the semi-darkness of early morning and I poured too much water into the flour. What was I to do? The shops were closed, there was no more flour, the dough was too soft to manipulate to make the dumplings - my brother liked them made very large; 'jacks', they were called. Thinking creatively, I extracted from the fireside the whitest ashes I could find, in the semi-darkness and with poor light from a lantern, and mixed it into the flour. Eventually I had put so much ash in with the flour that I was able to make the 'jacks'.

I fried and packed them for my brother, then went back to bed, leaving them for him to collect on his way to Inneswood. That night after returning from work, my brother asked, 'Joe, is what you do to de dumpling dem?'

'What you mean?', I innocently enquired.

'Well', he said, 'dem taste alright, but dem did black'.

What appeared to be white ashes were evidently not as white as it appeared in the semi-darkness of early morning with a lantern for light. It was many years later as an adult that I plucked up the courage to confess to my brother that I had put ashes in his dumplings! But my intentions were good.

My family, as I indicated above, were affected by migration. Two of my eldest brothers left for England around the same time as my father did, and I did not know them either until I arrived in the country at almost sixteen years old. Other siblings moved away from home with some visiting the USA for work. Over the years, my family became dispersed and living in three countries: Jamaica, England and the USA. Today one of us is deceased, five live in England, one in Jamaica, and four in the USA. Both mum and dad are deceased.

Notwithstanding this truncated upbringing, I still have fond and lasting memories of my childhood. Like the Saturday when mum went to Spanish town market to sell some of our produce, and left those of us who lived at home at the time to give ourselves the herbal 'washout' she regularly gave us to keep us healthy. It may have been good for our constitution, but herbs was the most distasteful drink that even passed my lips.

Anyway, on this particular day – and I do not recall which of us was the ringleader of the revolt - we decided that we were not going to drink this horrible tasting medicine since mum wasn't there to make us have it. Someone came up with the idea that we should give the whole pot of boiled herbs to the family pig that we kept tethered in the yard.

Well! Within a few hours that poor pig messed itself beyond description. It certainly had a wash out! When Saana returned it was standing in a very filthy place. She enquired what the matter with the pig was. None of us had any idea!

There were the trips I made with another of my brothers, Timothy, to Uppa Wood, for various reasons. On these trips, Timothy would try to educate me on a variety of topics. And to help me keep up with him as we walked he would sometimes tie a string to himself and to me, locating the string in our trouser belt fobs. On one occasion, the string broke and I began to lag behind. Timothy called out, 'walk up Joseph'. I began to raise my knees and my feet high off the ground thinking 'walk up' meant lifting my feet higher. Tim laughed and laughed.

Then one day I heard a man cursing some Jamaican 'bad words', swear words, and wanted to report to Timothy what I had heard. I instinctively knew I shouldn't say those words, so I asked him if I could spell them. Again Timothy laughed and laughed.

Timothy is the guitarist in the family and many were the home gatherings, usually impromptu, when we listened in awe as he fingerpicked his way around familiar songs, as we sang along. He taught me to play the guitar; a skill, thanks to him, I practise to this day; to amuse myself if no one else.

Another set of skills I learned growing up in Jamaica were tailoring ones. As a boy I spent time with the local tailor where I became a trusted assistant able to make buttonholes, create cuffs, and put the first crease in clients' new trousers. These were no mean feats because in that age of terralene trouser material you got one chance to make a crease in a new pair of trousers. Once made, the crease was permanent! To this day, I retain those skills; altering my trouser lengths and doing all my own ironing. This was to lead to an interesting deal struck with my young new bride!

When my second eldest brother, Lester, would make his 'coalskill' mounds at Uppa Wood, producing coal for sale at Spanish Town market; he would sometimes take me with him. We would leave home very early in the morning to check if all was well. A coalskill is a strange construct that take days to turn wood into coal under a mound where earth is used to cover a carefully crafted woodpile. Log and other suitable woods were the material my brother used in making coal.

At certain times of the year, we had the moon for light as Lester and I went on some of those early morning walks. As we wended our way through the narrow and winding path that led from home in Top Mountain to Uppa Wood, with due laden overhanging branches and leaves and tall grass; the sheer picturesque beauty left imprints in my mind. We could often times walk solely by moonlight.

Lester it was too who was the family's unrivalled storyteller. He would sit with us as night fell, under a big mango tree in our yard, and under the moonlight on clear evenings he would tell Anancy story after Anancy story. Some of those stories still live in my memory.

One of my favourite Anancy story Lester told us involved the fictional characters of Bra Anancy and Bra Tookuma. Bra Anancy was the trickster and Bra Tookuma the simpleton. In one story Bra Anancy visits Bra Tookuma and realises that Bra Tookuma has just cooked a pot of cornmeal porridge. Bra Anancy immediately wonders how he can dupe Bra Tookuma into giving him the lovely pot of porridge.

'Bra Tookuma', said Bra Anancy in Jamaican, 'you know say I can drink off dat pat a porridge hat hat so?'

Bra Tookuma shakes his head. 'If you can drink off the whol a dis pat a porridge Bra Anancy, you can have it'.

Bra Anancy picks up the pot, puts it to his mouth and the hot porridge burns his lips! But he doesn't flinch.

'But dis porridge no hat man', blurts Bra Anancy, 'lef it out in de sun mek it get a likkle hatta'.

And he does this repeatedly, until the porridge has cooled sufficiently so he could drink it all without taking the pot from his mouth.

Bra Anancy wipe his face clean and said, 'Bra Tookuma is what me did tell you? Me no did tell you say me can drink off de pat a porridge hat hat? It wasn't even hot enough fe me, till me have fi leave it ina de sun mek it get hatter'.

Bra Tookuma shakes his head, 'You bad you know Bra Anancy, you is a bad man'.

Cricket was a passion for me growing up in Jamaica. My pals and I played any and everywhere, with any and everything for equipment. I never saw a proper cricket ball, bat, pads, gloves or wicket for quite a while. We shaped the ends of dried coconut boughs and pieces of cut wood into bats. Young green oranges, limes and pieces of wood became cricket balls.

I never heard of pads or protective boxes and other cricketing paraphernalia until much later in life. We played cricket morning, noon and night. I still have an unrivalled and undying love for cricket – in spite of how poorly the West Indies cricket team may play these days. Later when I married, my new wife quickly realised she should not compete, so she learned the game and became a very good scorer, as well as having a knowledge of the sport. As school kids, we played timeless cricket tests that went on for days; before school, during recesses and after school. As a boy growing up, I couldn't get enough cricket.

If there was one thing guaranteed to get me into trouble it was my indulgence in playing or indeed watching cricket. One morning, Saana sent me to buy something from a shop in our district. En-route, I met upon some of my friends who were playing cricket. I joined in and played until nightfall!

Once again, Saana was not amused and sent for one of my elder brothers, Paul, to give me a beating. Paul came to do the job, but his intentions were a little too obvious. As he tried to grab hold of me I ran, he came after me and we ran for what seemed like miles. He gave up just before I was about to.

Later that night when I didn't return home - I actually hid in a tree close to our house, out of sight – there were audible mutterings that I had run away from home. My sisters turned on Paul holding him responsible for my presumed running away. I just waited until he left, then I crept back into our house and into bed. By morning it seemed mum had forgotten all about my misdemeanour of the day before. Such was the temporariness of Saana's rage.

If cricket was my weakness because of my love for the game, it was also the source of much pleasure. And I continued to devote much time to the game, even representing my school. I became a decent all-rounder, regularly opening the bowling in spite of my lack of height, and batting at six or seven in the batting order. Playing cricket continued in England with me representing college and church; playing whenever opportunity presented itself.

I had many experiences and acquired many skills while growing up in rural St Catherine, Jamaica; from activities that were natural in the context yet have helped equip me for life. These included cooking, fetching water in buckets, learning how not to let it splash; planting vegetables and watching them grow to maturation. Setting traps for birds, such as pringes and calabans, and shooting them out of trees with a catapult. We played marbles for cashew nuts as prizes, and lots more.

For whatever reason, I sometimes feel ashamed at how easily I was able to leave my friends behind when time came to migrate to England. May be it was because I was coming to join my parents and several siblings. Also, although I had many friends, I was an unnaturally shy child and always preferred family to friends; and since the bulk of family had moved to England it was not difficult to uproot to join them.

And yet I had special bonds with my boyhood friends. On a recent trip to Jamaica, one of them reminded me of an instance when we were young, when his mother made him return to their field near Uppa Wood for something important he had forgotten. It was getting dark and he was scared. I refused to allow him to go alone and volunteered to walk with him to and from his errand, as two little boys in the dark!

On occasions I refused to go into people's yards, I was even less inclined to go into their houses. Shy I may have been but I was not ashamed to join other children to run around naked in the rain. What was that about? I ask myself.

Some of my greatest life lessons were learned from my mother, Saana. There was a particular day when for our evening meal, all she had to feed her brood was a single stick of cassava. I can imagine the pent up love and frustration as she diligently peeled and cooked it, then she carefully cut it into enough segments so each of us and her could have a piece. There was nothing to eat with the little pieces of cassava except salt that we sprinkled on them and then drank lots of water.

We all ate without complaint. Saana took the occasion to tell us a story of our eldest brother, James, who by this time had migrated to the UK. On a day similar to this one, there wasn't enough food and everybody had a small portion. After James had eaten the morsel, he said, 'me belly no full but me satti'. That is, although his stomach was not filled (full), he was satisfied (satti). Saana wanted his to be our example and it was. The bible, she reminded us, says godliness with contentment is great gain.

Through this and other instances, Saana taught me how to be contented with less than what fills. Yet, my family was considerably better off than many in Top Mountain because our dad, Bra John, was in England sending remittances as often as he could. And Saana was industrious planting seeds on our plot of land. And still we struggled. I shudder to think how those in our district, without outside help, fared even for the basics of life. I do have an idea because in better times, many passed through our home at meal times and Saana would never turned anyone away hungry.

Apart from home and my neighbourhood, the other pillars of my upbringing were the church and school. Church and school came together for me at a very young age at what was called 'private school'. I now know that what I attended first was my local church's provision of nursery schooling.

In my district, there were three churches. A Wesleyan Holiness Church that seemed to attract the few posh people in the district. Their most memorable moment was a visit by a boy preacher who seemed to take the area by storm. I was young too but I remember still his mantra, 'some people sitting at God's dining table but dem can't eat at all'. I was not sure what he meant then and I am not sure now.

There was a Four Square Church in neighbouring Paul Mountain that never seemed to have more than ten members including the minister. He was also their only musician, on a banjo. In this sleepy church, suddenly news went round that Jesus' second coming was about to happen on a specific date. Almost all the people including the baddest men in Paul Mountain got religion, packed out the church for a few weeks until the predicted date passed without the parousia, the second coming. Things returned to normal.

Then there was the Church of God of Prophecy, my church. This was by a long way the largest of the three. My parents were members of this church when I was born, so I have been shaped spiritually by the teachings and culture of this church. Its doctrines were handed down from the United States, but its praxis and culture as I encountered them, were very rural Jamaican.

The local pastor, Deacon Altamont Richards, who I realised anon was not licensed by the church - just called Deacon and Pastor out of respect - because he didn't fulfil the church's requirement of being filled with the Holy Spirit evidenced by 'speaking in tongues', was a very impressive man. He seemed to me as a child well learned, articulate and intellectually head and shoulders above anyone else in the district. The postman who rode a bicycle into our district every other day always delivered the Jamaican Gleaner to Deacon Richard's home.

Not only was Deacon Richards not a deacon, he was not a pastor either. He permanently deputised, was proxy for an itinerant pastor who lived in nearby Spanish Town and visited once a month to serve communion, receive a report and pay. I admired Deacon Richards so much and was devastated to discover that the man I grew up believing was my pastor was so in name only. The ecclesial reasons only became clear to me later.

These things and much besides were lost on me as a child but I instinctively knew it was significant that the 'Pastor' often knelt in the altar seeking the 'baptism of the Holy Ghost' like the rest of us unfilled ones. We were kind of like the great unwashed! He did not kneel for long though; after a few minutes he would get up and sit in his special chair. The rest of us would kneel for what seemed like hours each time. I return to this doctrinal issue below.

It was great fun dressing up to go to church on Sundays, even if the 'Sunday best' often did not include a pair of shoes. And it was not only on Sundays that we went to church. In fact we went to church most nights. The question was about which night was 'rest night'. Church, alongside family and school was at the centre of my young existence.

It was at church that I was first exposed to speaking in front of a group of people, usually reciting a Sunday School 'golden text' from scripture, or giving a testimony about something that God had done. Occasionally I sang solo after it was discovered that I had a reasonable singing voice.

Everybody in our church was put in a band, a relic of the Methodist roots of holiness Pentecostalism, and my bandleader, Sister Vie, visited monthly. She would ask my mum, 'how is Bredda Joe getting on?' Mum would then proceed to tell on me of all my misdemeanours that month! Sister Vie was strict but gentle in her strictures; after all she didn't have many censoring options! She would usually make me promise to do better, and as a good Christian boy I would cooperate by always promising to do better. However, my Achilles heel, cricket, ensured that I would be back in the dock next month promising to do better again.

My main problem at church though was that, tarry as I might (the term 'tarry' meant to spend time in prayer asking God to fill one with the Holy Ghost, an interpretation given to Luke 24.49), I could not seem to get filled with the Holy Ghost with the evidence of speaking in tongues. My godmother, Sister Benny, seemed to have a deep and abiding desire to see her godson filled with the Spirit and used to encourage me to 'seek de Laad godson'.

In one early morning tarrying service – it seemed like tarrying was a form of punishment for the spiritually inadequate - I got caught up in the Spirit in trancelike fashion, but still did not speak in those illusive tongues. On the walk home, my godmother said to Saana, 'Joe just miss 'im blessin dis marning eeh?' Oh well, the tarrying was destined to continue.

Even as a child I felt condemned to going to early morning tarrying services to seek the blessing often referred to as the 'gift' of the Holy Ghost. A gift I was somehow not receiving. Oh boy, what a life! I was either waking up early to make fried dumplings for my brother, fetching water from a standpipe, fetching firewood, accompanying my brother to tend his coalskill at Uppa Wood or up early to go to the tarrying service. Little wonder I was up for going to England when the opportunity came.

For good or ill - sometimes both - church had a great impact on my life; so much so that aged eleven I had water baptism and became a full member of the Church of God of Prophecy. The Baptism followed my little sister Ruth and I deciding to have our last worldly dance under a naesberry tree and got saved, accepted Jesus as Saviour, that night. My understanding of faith then was juvenile.

I may well have needed saving because, young as I was, in addition to my many other sins, I was an ardent smoker of dried chocho and rosemary leaves. I was not alone. And I had a penchant for chasing mongooses with our family dogs and smoking them out of their holes to their deaths. Perversely, inflicting pain on animals did not faze me; and I sometimes cruelly stoned defenceless animals.

On one another occasion, my younger brother Jerry and I cornered and stoned a cat until we thought it was dead. We saw the cat the following day and wondered if it were a ghost! Then there is the time when a ram from a neighbouring herd of goats persistently bothered my young she goats. I laid in wait, took aim, and dealt it a severe blow on one of its hind legs. I took great delight in my direct hit as it hobbled away in obvious agony. In some ways I was a cruel child, in spite of my church's influence.

My first experience of school was my church's nursery school provision. My junior and primary school was Guanaboa Vale, St Catherine, about four miles from our family home. I remember well the journey to and from Guanaboa Vale School. It was a long walk, sometimes run, to school after the daily early morning chore alternating between water fetching, firewood fetching, animal tending or prayer meeting. Although the journey to school always followed some onerous chores, if you were late, you would be certain to get the cane from headmaster Montague.

It mattered not that none of us had clocks in our homes, there was one in the school by which the bell rang out on the stroke of 8.55am and 9am. If we were not in class by the time the second bell sounded, we were in trouble. On the way, we would gaze anxiously at the morning sun trying to discern whether we were on time or not. If we thought we were late, we sometimes resorted to a kind of group obeah, juvenile witchcraft, that was meant to call down malevolent spirits upon the headmaster and inhibit his ability to administer the cane.

We would get a piece of weed, and a stone, wrap the weed around the stone, say a few 'tongues' like we heard at church, call teacher Montague's name then toss the weed-wrapped stone behind us. This was supposed to lead to the head teacher's hand being suspended in the air as he raised it to hit us. Unfortunately, this act of necromancy never worked; but that never deterred us from repeating it whenever we suspected we were late and faced the ministry of the dreaded cane. This syncretisation of Christianity with African religion was quite telling for ones so young.

Fortunately, for residents from Top Mountain and its surrounding areas, schooling in Guanaboa Vale was short lived because, after less than a year attending there, a new all-age school opened in Paul Mountain. Almost all Top Mountain children went there. A few pupils went to the nearby Kitson Town all-age school. Instead of the long haul to Guanaboa Vale, I now had a walk to school of about a mile. It felt like it was on my doorstep.

And the new school was a stone's throw from our family plot, Outa Road, in Paul Mountain. Not far to go to collect Number Eleven mangoes and other fruits at break times as we did often. The head teacher at Paul Mountain School, Winston Chambers, was very much like Montague from Guanaboa Vale. Both loved to use the cane, as was the culture at the time. In fact at the opening of the new school, the visiting school inspector presented head teacher Chambers with a gift. It was a thick leather strap that the inspector named, 'Doctor Do Me Good'! Eventually teacher Chambers tired of the strap and resorted to specially cut supple jack whips from the hill by the school.

The big boys had responsibility for discipline in the school under Chambers' instructions and so they got to fetch the supple jacks. This worked well most of the time, but the head boys knew that they were not necessarily exempt from a whipping; and sometimes, mischievously, screwed the joints of the whips so they would not last too long. On one occasion, teacher chambers spotted the whips were perishing rather quickly with use, so he tested one by bending it and spotted what had happened. He summoned the head boys to the front of the class and used up all six whips on them! They never screwed whip joints again.

An early high point at the new Paul Mountain School was celebrating Jamaica's independence from British rule on the 6th of August 1962. Without knowing much of the significance of Independence, we were all well rehearsed for renditions of the new anthem and national prayer during a whole day of independence celebrations. There I was vigorously waving my Jamaican Flag and singing on what we all knew was a momentous day; only many years afterwards has the reality of what it means for Jamaica to be an independent nation dawned on me.

Even after fifty years of independence, Jamaica continues to hold the Queen of England as its Head of State. For reasons still not entirely clear to me, I favour Republicanism over Monarchy. I find myself wishing Jamaica had a Jamaican Queen. My republican tendencies are, however, without much practical significance since as a Jamaican living abroad I would not have a vote were Jamaica to hold a referendum on the issue, as has been mooted in recent times.

My favourite teacher at Paul Mountain was Mrs Douse who seemed to have been on a mission to educate and inculcate moral values in her pupils. She taught us some important life lessons in rhyme. I remember some to this day and have taught them to my children:

Speak the truth and speak it ever
Cost it what it will
He who hides the wrong he did
Does the wrong thing still
and
He who would strive must rise at five
He who has striven may stay till seven
He is a thriftless loon who lies until eleven.

Mrs Douse was a brilliant teacher who made me fall in love with arithmetic, particularly 'long divisions'. Dividing numbers nowadays is made easy with the use of electronic calculators, but back in the 1960s in rural Jamaica, applying your brain aided by paper and pencil; or chalk and chalkboard, was the only way. I was a reasonably bright child, doing well in Geography, Maths and English. I even learned a little Latin and some Spanish too.

I loved reading and discovering the meaning of words. Treasure Island by Robert Louis Stephenson was a favourite. As was Gulliver's Travels. The mighty Gulliver being outmanoeuvred by the little people in the story of 'Gulliver in the Land of Little People' taught me something about how the efforts of the many can subdue the powerful one.

I was friends with both Mrs Douse' son, and head teacher Chambers' son, both of whom were about my age. We made a formidable team, helping each other with studies and might have been seen as those destined for academic success. Fortunately too, although corporal punishment was a staple recourse for teachers, particularly so for head teacher Chambers, I escaped with very few brushes with the strap or the whip. This may have had something to do with the company I kept! Corporal punishment tends to be viewed extremely negatively in social circles nowadays, and I never enjoyed it on the few occasions it was visited upon me back then. I never liked it being perpetrated upon anyone else either, and I am no apologist for it now. However, one way of understanding it in the post slavery, colonial Jamaican education context I grew up in, is as part of a structure of strict sometimes brutal discipline in schools.

Few would disagree that learning happens best within a framework of cultural affirmation and discipline; but discipline should not be synonymous with corporal punishment. Not that school in Paul Mountain was reduced to that. There was a clear curriculum; timekeeping was very important and enforced by the threat of corporal punishment; school uniform was compulsory. My khaki trousers and shirt had to be immaculately presented at the start of each week. Even when my clothes were soiled, they had to be neat!

So the use of the cane or the whip did not occur in isolation, although having said that I believe there was more than a touch of masochism evident in some teachers. The resort to beating, and the extent of such beatings, was often and cruel. I witnessed one school friend beaten by a teacher to the extent that when the beating was over, the child was scooped off the floor and taken to hospital. I doubt that the possibility of action against the teacher was considered by anyone. 'Spare not the rod and spoil the child', seemed to have been taken very literally. Alongside this was strict adherence to holding prayers at the start of every day of schooling. The worship of God in a sometimes cruel setting tended to domesticate the divine as a cruel disciplinarian.

Paul Mountain School was divided into 'houses' that competed against each other especially on sports days; at cricket, baseball and other sports. On a famed day of the cricket competition, my Custus House was pitted against my best mate and cousin Palo's. I opened the bowling and he opened the batting for his house. I ran in with purpose but Palo hit my first ball, the first of the match, for six onto the roof of the school. His smug face looked down the wicket at me as though to say, 'got you'. I just thought, 'how dare you?'

No opening bowler enjoys being hit for six first ball – even if he is only 5' 6" - so my running in to bowl the next ball was mixed with anger and fear that he might hit my second ball for six. Palo had a reputation as a bit of a dasher. But I was bent on vengeance. 'I'm coming to get you'. My second ball was a yorker on middle stump which Palo attempted to do as he did first ball; but this time he missed it completely and his middle stump was sent cartwheeling out of the ground. My joy was unbounded! To this day whenever Palo and I meet, we rehearse that cameo performance. I have no recollection how the match resulted.

My reputation as an opening bowler grew and I was picked to play for my school against neighbouring Kitson Town School. On the day of the match, the Kitson Town boys arrived. They looked like giants compared to us, especially me. I was petrified. I quietly slipped away into the hillside close to the school. They couldn't find me and I presumed they replaced me and continued the match, which I watched from the safety of the hillside.

This was not the only time I hid from action. I did the same when a van bringing nurses to vaccinate the children in school. I decided no way was I going to take any injection that day, so off to the hill I went until the medical van left. I am still a reluctant subject to the injection needle and can honestly say I have never seen a needle that injected me to this day.

My eyes are closed as soon as I sit in the chair!

At school I also boxed, and was not bad boxer either. As was the case with other sports, we never had very much by way of proper equipment. So too with boxing, fellow pupils would form a ring by holding hands, one would act as referee, and two children would box each other bare handed. I was a stylist and always tried to out manoeuvre my opponents without taking too many hits.

Though an artful boxer, I was not particularly brave and on more than one occasion my siblings had to come to my defence or I would have been beaten up by other children.

Life was a constant challenge in one sphere or another. For example, my church taught as a mark of holy living, against members participating in 'professional ball games'. This was interpreted by my local church as ball games that were played professionally. Consequently, cricket, football, volleyball and rounders were all forbidden to church members. I instinctively knew or conveniently believed that such a teaching that denied a boy the pleasure of playing the beautiful game of cricket was oppressive and wrong. So notwithstanding the teaching of my church I persisted in playing but also knew I had to be discreet.

One way around my quandary was enlisting my mates as 'look out' that should any member of my church appear on the horizon of wherever we happen to be playing, they would alert me and I would run for cover, returning when they indicated to me it was safe. It was most important that my bandleader didn't see me playing cricket or any other ball games because I would be promising yet again to do better.

There were other church teachings and advice that, as I grew older, I found challenging, and later in life would challenge both openly and covertly. No one were allowed to wear shorts in public? Or go swimming where men and women used the same bathing area? Or go to the theatre or cinema? Or wear gold for ornament? No doubt, there must have been some sound advice too but I do not recall them now. I played a good and effective game of hide and seek with my church.

As I approached my fifteenth birthday, attentions began to turn towards the national Common Entrance Exams, which one had to pass to go to one of Jamaica's high schools. I was fully expected to pass, but I failed; marginally I was told and needed to do a re-sit. However, by now my attention was turning to immigrating to England to join the rest of the family that had gone there, including mum. I did not know it at the time, but the urgency with me concerned my age. If I were to join my parents as a minor, I needed to go before my sixteenth birthday. No resits were going to be allowed to get in my way. England beckoned.

I acted as a mature fifteen year old travelling to and from Spanish Town and Kingston to process my travel documents preparing to fly to England. I surprised myself at how adept I quickly became at those things. Having been born and bred in the country with scarcely any of life's fineries I very much enjoyed spending time in the air conditioned facilities of the passport office, travel agents, and other related places of travel business.

I took opportunities to visit a few people who had migrated from our country district to Spanish Town and Kingston, including one of my sisters, Cynthia and my brother Timothy. It was at Cynthia's flat in Spanish Town that I first flicked a light switch. Having successfully processed my travel documents, I flew to England on 27 September 1968, bright-eyed and bushy tailed on the BOAC plane that landed at Heathrow, London the following morning. Arriving that day I was dressed in the very first suit I had ever owned, a felt cap, and other clothes my family had bought me as going away presents.

I said farewell to cousins, elder brothers and sisters, friends Mendis, Austin, Edwin and Selvin and many more; consoled in the knowledge I was on my way to meet up again with my mother, my father, brothers and sisters some of whom I hardly knew. It did not occur to me that I would ever return to Jamaica, even as a visitor. It felt like a one-way ticket.

CHAPTER 2

From Smethwick to Marriage 1968-1974

It was a fine sunny September's evening when I boarded the BOAC airplane at Kingston's Palisadoes Airport, Jamaica; but it was a cold and dismal September's morning when I landed at Heathrow Airport, London, England after an overnight flight. It was my first flight ever on an aeroplane – in fact, I had never left the island before - a strange yet unscary experience. It never occurred to me to be scared of flying, although I have developed something of a phobia since. I had never seen an airplane close up before, let alone fly in one; I had only ever seen them fly overhead in Top Mountain as we lived in the flight path for planes landing in Kingston.

Having disembarked at Heathrow, I was met by three men, none of whom I recognised. They turned out to be Bra John, my father; my eldest brother, James and a family friend, Stanford Fletcher. Meeting my father properly for the first time at the age of (almost) sixteen was strange. Although I knew the significance of his being my dad, to a great extent he was in the same place as the other men with him, they were strangers. The person I looked forward to seeing again the most was my mum Saana, but for that I had still to wait. And that was going to be after the longest car ride I had ever had in my entire life.

Eventually, arriving in Birmingham, the first house I was taken to was that of my brother James and his wife Daisy. It was an emotional meeting as I was reunited with Saana, my younger siblings, sisters Ruth and Winsome, and brother Jerry, all of whom had left me behind in Jamaica a year earlier. It was late afternoon to early evening by the time I got to James' house. Having met and made a fuss of and by everybody, I began to feel at home again with a significant part of my family. Although some faces were new, this felt like home from home.

I proceeded to take off my clothes, all of which were new and I had been in them for over a day since I left Top Mountain for Kingston the day before. After a day's travel by land and air I had become quite uncomfortable. I stripped down to my vest (marina, as Saana called it), underpants, having removed everything else including socks. I had been accustomed to spending the majority of my time out of doors, so I instinctively headed for the back door; only to be hauled back inside with the accompanying familiar voice of Saana, 'Josive! Come back inside. Is what you tink you doing? Eh? You tink is Jamaica dis?'

Welcome to England Joseph! It was autumn, and although I was not allowed to remain outside to find out, it was chilly and not a bit like the Jamaican country side I had just left the day before.

Having arrived in England on a Saturday, Sunday and church soon came. Familiar territory. Less predictable, however, was that my mother had decided to submit my name to sing in a fundraising concert (called a programme) on my very first Sunday night in England. I still cannot recall if she asked, or even told me before submitting my name. She was keen to show off her son who had sung a few times at our Top Mountain church in Jamaica. I had no idea she thought I was a good singer.

At some stage between arriving in England on Saturday and Sunday night's programme at my new local church at Peel Street, Winson Green, Saana hinted that she had put my name forward to sing in the programme. I was not fazed by this; she knew me well enough as a complex mix of shyness and bravado. The extent to which my Top Mountain upbringing had prepared me for the world was beginning to unfold. I had never rehearsed with a band, ever, and did not have any song prepared for rendition. But I was going to sing because my proud mother had said I would. I decided to sing a song I had heard sung in church in Jamaica, though I had never sung it solo before. It was No.106 from our church hymnal, the Banner Hymns, titled 'Dear Jesus I'm coming to see you some day'.

Sunday night came and the programme got started. Soon my name was called and I was introduced as Brother and Sister Aldred's son who came from Jamaica just the day before. I walked shyly to the front, before a congregation that looked almost exactly like the one I was used to in Top Mountain, if now a little overdressed. I opened the Banner Hymns and began to sing, totally unrehearsed. The music band quickly began to play along and the three stanzas and chorus repeated after each one were done before I knew. And I could not have imagined what followed.

The congregation erupted in a chorus of 'encore, encore, encore'. Money came pouring in for me to sing the song again. There was such excitement. I was completely swept up in the euphoria the like of which I had not experienced before. When the din had died down I sang it again. If the chorus of 'encore' was any less than the first, I did not notice. More money poured in while the musicians played and the people rejoiced. They had found a new singing star, fresh from Jamaica. I sang a second encore and could easily could have sung a third, given the buzz that still pervaded. From that night, my first Sunday in England, my career as a gospel singer was launched.

Back in the 1960s and 1970s, the Church of God of Prophecy to which I belonged did not mix much with other churches and did not encourage members to do so either. And so my singing never got much beyond my own denomination and a few churches similar in type. For many years I sang solo and as part of a group called 'The Spiritual Rhythms'. Even today after years of wider ministry people in my local church with long memories still mention my singing, and some feel cheated I do not still perform.

But something else happened on my first Sunday in church that threatened to dampen my mood. I was all dressed up in the suit I had worn from Jamaica, including my felt hat as I arrived at my new church for the very first time. I left my hat in a porch area where hats and coats seemed to have been left by many people. At the close of the service as we prepared to leave I went in search of my new hat - it was gone! And I never saw it ever again. My thought process went something like, 'people steal in church?' That was a sobering lesson and one I tried to learn about human nature in and out of church, always take care of your stuff!

Living accommodation was to prove challenging. Our dad Bra John never bought a house, and his bachelor pad went when Saana and the other children arrived a year before. But they were still in temporary accommodation. My arrival further complicated matters and we lived in two places for my first few days in England. My brother and his wife had children of their own in their Smethwick three-bed semi-detached home where first I came; I soon discovered that this was not where I would be living. Soon we all moved into Brother Stanford Fletcher's large terraced house in a nearby part of Smethwick where my parents had been staying.

Mine was an attic room which I shared with my brother Jerry. Later I was to feel somewhat disappointed that my parents did not own a house; because although the Fletcher's were childless, and they were very accommodating, their house with the six of our family alone was rather crowded. In the thirteen years my father had lived and worked in England he had not managed to save enough to buy a house because of having to pay rent, regularly send money back home to look after us, pay the air fares for the two eldest brothers to join him in England, my mum's two trips, and of course the four of us who came later.

We did not have to live long in the cramped conditions at Brother Fletcher's house, because our application for a council flat was successful and we moved into a lovely maisonette in Hawkins Court, Oldbury Road, Smethwick. Although I still had to share a room with younger brother Jerry, at least it was not in an attic! Since those halcyon days, local people have taken to calling the estate on which Hawkins Court is situated 'Concrete Jungle'; but for me, it felt like living in Buckingham Palace. And compared with our 'detached' home facilities in Top Mountain, this was quite a step up with all conveniences under one roof, electricity, running water, a gas cooker, carpets, dining room table, settees: this was a welcome change.

I had not passed my Common Entrance Exam in Jamaica before coming to England, and after a few months I had by now turned sixteen so was too old to go to school. I was at an uncertain point in relation to the English education system.

But I soon discovered that I was far from alone. Many children caught up in the migration of our parents seeking improved economic conditions for their families were in the same situation as me. Many of us had arrived just in time to beat the sixteen year old ceiling of minors joining parents, and our education had suffered as a consequence of the focus on the expediency of getting to England.

It was decided that I should enrol at Bourneville College of Further Education. This was all a stepped change from life in Top Mountain. I now got up early not to tend the family animals, fetch water, firewood or attend early morning prayer meetings, but to catch the No.87 bus, then the No.82, then the No.11 to get to Bourneville before 9am! So many pieces of clothes to wear to keep warm including a heavy coat. And the mornings were dark! At least there was not the threat of the cane if I were late.

At Bourneville, I met others just like me and formed a kind of unofficial young migrants' gang. The educators at Bourneville, did not know what to do with us and put us in a kind of remedial class together where we were being taught the basics of English and Arithmetic.

Someone must have noticed that the abc stuff they were teaching us were significantly below the abilities of some of us, and I, with others, was put in the O Level group half way through the academic year. I studied Maths, English, Geography and Commerce but found the English teaching system very challenging; joining half way through the year didn't help either. At the end of the second year, I sat the O Level exams in the four subjects and; let's say I didn't do as well as I had been expected to do. Well enough though to get a job in the Telephone Manager's office.

While it was not too strange that I performed badly in Commerce and Geography, since the former was a new subject to me and the latter had a very different focus to the curriculum in Jamaica, it was a real surprise to me that I did not get high grades in Maths and English, subjects I excelled in back in Jamaica. I did not get grades sufficient to go on to A Level and then University. Saana was particularly disappointed and must have wondered what had happened to the bright schoolboy who used to come home from Paul Mountain School with books piled high upon his arm. I know mother was disappointed because, although she didn't say much to me, she told our new Pastor, Bishop McCalla, who visited the home and expressed his commiserations and hope that I would continue my studies.

I wanted to return to Bourneville to redo my O Levels to achieve higher grades, but it was felt that I needed to get a job to help support the home. I enquired if I might do resits immediately and was allowed to re-sit English which without much revision I gained a higher grade in. This meant much to me because it confirmed what I believed, that had I had time to adjust to the new English education system I could have passed its exams with high grades.

Alas! It was not to be and I got a job as a statistics clerk in the Telephone Manager's Office on Broad Street in Birmingham. In the coming months and years I would attempt a number of education initiatives, including learning to touch type; something I was never very good at but as is evidenced by this self-typed work, I am reasonably proficient – even though my typing involves my two index fingers in the main!

At Bourneville College I may not have fulfilled my academic potential but I quickly made my mark as a cricketing all-rounder and a badminton player. The tutors soon discovered my pretty brisk medium paced bowling and number 6 batting and drafted me in to play for the staff who were mostly older men. My best returns playing for the staff team was seven for thirty six, in a match we still managed to lose! I had never played badminton before, but within a year I was the second best player in the college, bettered only by a former national champion junior player from Kenya, whose name escapes me.

Bourneville is memorable for many more reasons. It was a well-manicured place as befitting a site owned by the wealthy Cadbury's family and sitting next door to the Cadbury's factory that attracted many visitors owing to famous chocolate making – I loved Cadbury's chocolates, especially marathon chocolate and nut bars.

I made lots of friends at the college some of whom I am in touch with still, and periodically I meet someone from that time.

One of those friends while at the college wrote something on the blackboard that struck a chord and has remained with me: 'a house of fools feeding on froth'. I believe he was summing up his thoughts on the quality of the education we were receiving at the college in what seemed like a remedial class.

Probably my most significant memory of Bourneville is a spiritual one. Having been a church boy from birth – my family had been members of the Church of God of Prophecy when I was born – baptised at eleven years of age and a mostly obedient, if sometimes dissident, adherent to the codes of my church, I had not realised how little my faith was based on real personal convictions. Still a teenager and with fellow teenagers around me keen to have a good time, I found myself reluctant to 'let my hair down' and engage in some of the activities they did.

Some of the young people I attended Bourneville College with back in the early 70s were quite hedonistic and challenged my rather conservative style of faith. Questions, asked and implied, demanded to know why I did not curse and swear, chase girls and party like they did.

I needed, for them and for me, a rationale for my refusal to run with the pack. It was a crisis moment as I tried to differentiate between what I did or did not do because my church said so, and what I did or did not do based on what I was convinced God required. It was easy enough to relate to my church because I could see and hear its requirements; but God? What did God require and how was I to know? Here is the rub: did I really believe in God, or was I merely keeping up a facade, church custom and tradition? I went into a period of deep thought.

The theory of evolution was little known to me, but I knew enough to reflect on whether the universe came about by chance or by a divine act? I reflected upon the complexity of the universe, the human body, and life on earth. I concluded that there simply has to be a creator, an architect and sustainer to this complex design. I also concluded that my behaviour should honour God; which was not the same as running with 'the pack' of my friends or unquestioningly obeying my church. Believing in God as opposed to believing in Church was and remains quite liberating.

My very first job was as a part-time attendant at P J Hylton petrol station in Oldbury near to where we lived. This was during my time as a student at Bourneville College. That was my first introduction to 'forbidden' glossy magazines for men that were kept on the top shelves and my introduction to knowing that just because the dispenser was labelled 'distilled water' for your car battery, did not mean it was 'distilled water'. Let the reader understand!

My first proper job after Bourneville College, circa 1972, as a clerk in the Telephone Manager's office on Broad Street, Birmingham city centre allowed me quite some flexibility. In between doing some actual work, I spent much time on the telephone chatting to friends and at lunch times playing table tennis, which I quickly learned to play reasonably well.

The telephone conversations were free because this was the Post Office and my main conversationalist was a Post Office telephonist. At that time the Post Office ran British telecommunications and we were employees. Free telephone conversations with friends was a bonus for doing a pretty mundane job. It's fair to say that although I liked arithmetic, collating statistics on how many telephone calls were being made between Coseley and Bewdley, for example, in order to help decide whether more or less lines were needed failed to excite me after a month in the job.

My mother Saana though was very impressed with her son dressing up in a shirt and tie every day to go to work. For her I had a 'proper job'. And my modest income helped with the family budget. Years later Saana was to tell me that this was the best job I ever had! I soon began to dream about what I really wanted to do with my life. Bright but with little qualification and rough around the edges socially and having left deep rural life in Jamaica less than four years ago, my options were not many. For some inexplicable reason I thought of becoming a post office clerk - I could imagine myself behind a post office counter. I thought about becoming a computer programmer. But my biggest impression was that of becoming a salesman. I have no idea why.

As ever, life is multi-dimensional and even as I was contemplating education and employment choices, I was forming relationships with young ladies. Three stories come to mind. I was invited to a bonfire night by a young woman from our local church. She was a little older than me and a little more worldly-wise. As we walked around the fireworks and amusements, she held and kissed me in a way no one had before. She seemed to sense my clumsiness, if not my reluctance, pulled back and said, 'have you never kissed a girl before?' I hadn't and that was the end of that.

On another occasion, I was travelling in the rear of a car which was dropping off a number of people to their homes. Suddenly I was alone with this young woman in the back seat with only the driver in the front. I began to feel my way toward this young lady in an intentionally romantic manner. I still recall the cold response and a look I could 'feel' that rebuked me in no uncertain way. I knew she was having none of it.

Then there was, who I shall call Sadie (not her real name), with whom I really was mutually romantically linked. We spent many courting moments in the beautiful Botanical Gardens and other places of interest. I really thought this was it and we would eventually marry. I was of course still very young, still a teenager, and the relationship was becoming serious and beginning to veer towards the kind of intimacy that would almost certainly result in full sexual intercourse – something strictly forbidden by my faith outside of marriage. After one particular incident at her parents' home, we broke off the relationship. Neither of us was in a position to do anything other than get the other into trouble!

I met and was growing up with a group of young men and women at church who were to become life-long pals and who over the years since our youth have had a tremendously influential impact upon my life. The bible is correct to valorise good friends (Proverbs 18.24). These friends have stayed together as we have pursued careers, sought to better understand our faith, tested the parameters of doing business together and apart, been there at moments of personal crises and some of us, in particular three couples self-styled 'the fab six', still meet periodically to 'put the world to right'.

With one of my best friends, and I have had and still have quite a few, I even tested out going into business with. George was a Medical Engineer at a local hospital and I was a well-established salesperson so we decided to market scissor-sharpening to local barbers and hairdressers. We will never know whether we might have succeeded since although it looked like taking off, I was called away to my first pastorate far away; something to which I will return later.

My call to ministry, if there was ever a particular point in time when this happened, was probably at aged seventeen. I was asked by my Sunday School teacher, Sister Watson, to help to teach the Sunday School class I was a part of. I can only imagine that I asked too many questions and this was her way of tapping into my curiosity. Maybe she thought she spotted real talent. Whatever her reasons, it was a significant move because at around this time a new pastor, Bishop McCalla, arrived at our church and immediately took an interest in the spiritual and social life and aspirations particularly of the young men.

Pastor McCalla was a dynamic man who clearly wanted us to aspire - the lads in his church certainly were pushed more than the girls; something from which I benefited significantly over the years. The mothers in the church also took an interest in me; inviting me to prayer meetings and asking me to give exhortations. There was the Sunday School superintendent, Brother Watson, who teased us with questions he alone knew the answers to. Gradually, the combination of a mother who wanted me to do well, a pushy pastor, challenging Sunday School teaching, a singing ministry, and homilies in prayer meetings meant I began to emerge as a person with ministry potential in my local church.

My emerging ministry was not only spiritual. I was instrumental, with other young men, in establishing a cricket team at our church that kept us lads occupied in physical exercises. Once again my medium paced bowling and middle order batting found expression!

Whilst still working at the Telephone Manager's Office I decided to act upon two things simultaneously. I enrolled with the National School of Salesmanship and started to investigate how I could become a computer programmer. My mother, always ambitious for me, agreed to borrow the money for me to study computing although she strongly disagreed with my plan to leave my clerical assistant job at the Telephone Manager's Office. I signed up to study COBOL computer programming which necessitated a move to London.

I continued studying with the National School of Salesmanship by correspondence, left my job at the Telephone Manager's Office and moved to London to learn COBOL programming with what I now know was a private company, in the hope of breaking into the emerging computing industry. It was all a great adventure for me just a few short years since coming to England. I seem to have taken to life in my new country like a duck to water.

I have to admit though that a factor in wanting to leave home was that my father and I never really got along. Arriving in England at almost sixteen years old, I realised that Bra John was rather inclined to the use of corporal punishment and made it clear to me that if I didn't obey him he would beat me. I made it known to my mother that if he hit me I couldn't guarantee I wouldn't hit him back. From then there existed a kind of father son standoff. Cordial, but with an undercurrent of tension.

The situation was not helped by my tendency to stay out late with my friends, and on more than one occasion, we crossed at the front door as he made his way to do his 6am-2pm shift and I was just coming home! We lived an uneasy truce. Mother was an excellent go-between and father never tried to beat me. My younger siblings didn't have the same luck.

I enjoyed London, where the estranged wife of one of my brothers lived and ensured I was well fed and watered. I visited her home most weekends I was in London and sometimes during the week. Whilst attending classes I worked part-time in a supermarket store and had a whale of a time munching on the foodstuffs I was supposed to be packing. I have no idea whether I was allowed to eat some of the things I ate.

Still acclimatising to life in England, London added to my steep learning curve. Initially I lived in digs, without the comforts of the family home. For food, I discovered Wimpy, one of the forerunners in fast-food, and ate there so often it was ridiculous. It wasn't long before, having discovered the local Church of God of Prophecy congregation, I was encouraged to move in with a church family. The Edwards' were more than I could have hoped for. The Pastor of the church, Rev'd Vera Rodney, took me into her heart and her home, and my singing endeared me to her congregation. I spent a lot of time at her family home and learned a salutary lesson from her after a sobering experience.

One night I was walking home to my room at the Edwards' home when a car slowed beside me. A black man peeked out of the window and asked if I knew a particular street. I did and told him so. He then asked me if I minded showing him where it was. Being the naïve country bumpkin I clearly still was, I said OK and hopped into his car's front passenger seat. I cannot recall the conversation, but he drove past the street and I asked him why he didn't stop.

He continued driving and for the first time I began to get concerned that I was being abducted; but as my concern grew, he said he was merely driving to turn his car around. He then pulled up outside what turned out to be his own home. In my innocent country boy just come to town way, I did not even find it strange he was asking for a street so close to where he lived. I opened the door and began to walk towards my own home.

The man then asked me if I minded coming in for a drink and I said OK. In this man's house, he invited me to sit down on a settee. I did. He disappeared into another room and before long re-emerged from the room, stark naked. I became concerned about what this might mean. I asked the man why he didn't put some clothes on and he went back to the room and returned wearing a dressing gown.

He offered me a cup of tea, came and sat down and began to tell me a sob story about how his marriage had broken down, and his family was in some kind of disarray. By now I realised I needed to leave this man's house, but how I did not know. Somehow, I had the presence of mind to tell him I was a Christian and asked if he would like me to pray for him. He said yes and I asked him to kneel down. As he did, I rushed to the door as fast as I could and out the front door I ran. Fortunately for me the doors were not bolted.

The following day I visited Pastor Rodney and told her the story. Her immortal words were, 'Joseph, are you a fool? Why you went in that man's house at that time of the night? You know he could have had other men there with him? You know he could have raped you?' This was the first time I had ever heard of male rape. I reasoned I had had a lucky escape!

My learning COBOL computer language was very slow! And I finished stage one of the course but was not at all certain this was for me – although Saana had borrowed money to send me on this course. She was not going to be pleased if I dropped out. I persevered but was not offered a job as I had been more or less promised.

My correspondence course with the National School of Salesmanship was going well though and offered some light at the end of a murky tunnel. I needed to return to my parents' home in Smethwick since the reason for which I had gone to London had now come to an end. I never quite caught the London bug of needing to live in the big city, probably because as a former country boy, Birmingham and the Black Country was sufficient an exposure to urban life.

I had made some friends in London in the months I had been there, one of whom was to become my best man at my wedding; Pastor Rodney, her family and her congregation and the Edwards family had been very supportive; my sister-in-law had fed me well; but the overwhelming majority of my meaningful relationships including my nuclear family, friends and local church were back in Birmingham. In this somewhat mixed moment something was about to happen that would revolutionise my life for ever; I met my future wife!

One of the young ladies I had met while in London, Rose, invited me to a revival service at the Church of God of Prophecy at Tubbs Road, Harlesden, London. My growing reputation as a gospel singer with an interest now in playing the bass was spreading, and the invitation may well have been with a view to my singing in that night's service. I do not recall whether I did or not that night. However, I was in close proximity to the music band.

During the lively music and singing I noticed a diminutive and beautiful young lady in one section of the hall. She had on a puffy blue and white cap with a button on top and with all of the singing, music, praying and preaching that went on that night my attention was on one person only. At the close of the service, I asked Rose if she could introduce me to the young lady; she did. As we stood on the pavement outside the church, Rose introduced me to Novelette who turned out to be a friend of hers.

My opening chat up line was terrible. In addition to disputing much of what I recall of that evening, my wife Novelette tells me that I said, 'you are so raving ugly'. I meant the total opposite, of course. It was a clumsy attempt at irony or mild sarcasm. Novelette, however, was not amused and it took quite some time and some fleet of foot friendly diplomacy by Rose before she would engage with me. I managed to get Novelette's telephone number! That was enough for me, on the cusp of returning to Birmingham.

I know, because Novelette told me so, that it was not love at first sight for her. It was for me, and having moved back to Birmingham the ensuing months saw me spending a lot of time and money in a telephone kiosk located on the corner of Oldbury Road and Spon Lane, Smethwick. There were times when the kiosk malfunctioned so that Novelette and I spoke for hours for free. Thanks British Telecom.

Novelette was a slender sixteen year old when we met and just out of school; I was nineteen. She worked as a telephonist and had, and still has, the most beautiful telephone voice and personality one could ever wish to hear. A mixture of lengthy, frequent telephone conversations, infrequent trips to London, occasional meetings at church conventions meant that our romance developed gradually. Here was I, a mere three years since arriving in England dating someone who at least in my mind was destined to be the love of my life. It would not be all plain sailing.

Back in Birmingham I was again with my family, local church and the friends I had met since coming from Jamaica. Various options opened up to my precocious approach to life. One of the first thing I did upon returning to Birmingham was to learn to drive. A brother from the Wolverhampton Church of God of Prophecy, Brother Millen, had a driving school and I enrolled with him. Between paid lessons I would get some practice from driving one of my friends' car.

After a late night chatting session between us lads, Gee was taking me home and I persuaded him to again let me drive. We didn't put on the L Plate and as I drove a police car appeared behind me. I came to a stop at traffic lights in West Bromwich and struck with nerves I stalled the car as I pulled away. My worst fears were realised when the blue lights started flashing and the police indicated I should stop. For not displaying an L Plate, Gee and I were both booked; fined with points on both licences. Gee's generosity did not deserve that outcome.

Soon my driving instructor decided I was ready to apply for my test. Although I stalled the car once during the test drive, I remembered what to do if that happened, and I passed the test - first time! Brother Millen taught me I can get a car through the eye of a needle if I keep my nerves.

My course with the National School of Salesmanship was very successful. I passed with flying colours – I am not sure if anybody was allowed to fail. True to their word in their ad, that if successful they guarantee you job interviews, I was sent on some interviews. One was with a company called the American Photocopying Equipment Company Ltd; APECO for short. Based on Mucklows Hill, Halesowen; the sales manager decided to take a punt on me as a trainee sales executive.

I realise now that back then in circa 1973 that was a major risk and I soon learned about the existence of racism as well as the opportunities to exploit race to one's benefit. APECO gave me the opportunity to get into sales that I had long coveted; with a company car and a salary. The training was intensive, both on the job and listening to a series of training tapes by a man called Mr Van Rees.

Via the audio tapes I learned how to canvass, get leads, make appointments with the right person with power to purchase, demonstrate photocopiers, close deals and do customer follow-up. One of Mr Van Rees' more memorable phrases was, 'put yourself in danger of making a sale. Get out of the office and meet people'. I followed Van Rees sales technique closely as well as the tips I picked up in my correspondence course.

APECO marketed wet toner photocopiers which were on display in the Halesowen showroom, and when pre-arranged would be taken in my ford estate car to office venues for demonstration. At my first Christmas office party with APECO, I invited my pastor's daughter to accompany me. She could have only been fourteen at the time, but had the advantage of appearing older than she was, especially in an evening dress. Apparently this created in some quarters an expectation that we would marry eventually; this in spite of the seven year difference in our respective ages. This was not my intention and I doubt marriage had entered her young thoughts either, but I suppose dating the pastor's daughter was bound to raise some eyebrows.

I continued to work for APECO until the company went into liquidation and made all staff redundant. At a stroke I lost my prestigious job with salary and car, and at a most inconvenient time in my life. Working as a young black salesman with APECO was a real eye-opener for me.

The sales process involved walking armed with the company's brochures, pen and paper, looking for likely commercial and industrial customers. Once identified, I would go to reception, ask the name of the person responsible for buying; note the name and contact number, then leave the promotional material with the receptionist to be passed on to the buyer.

After a week I would telephone the buyer on my telethon day, enquire if he or she had received the information I left for them, and whether there was an interest in discussing further their company's photocopying needs. Where an appointment was successfully made I would prepare to visit to discuss the company's needs, a machine demonstration and possibly a trial period of a suitable photocopier.

A recurring theme whilst I worked for APECO was that I would turn up to a prearranged meeting that I had arranged and would be met by a surprised look and occasionally by the statement, 'we were expecting Mr Aldred' or the question, 'are you Mr Aldred?'. It took me in my innocence a while to realise that the problem was that they did not expect a black man. Had I lost my Jamaican rural accent so swiftly?

My singing and music talents continued to make an impact at my church. My father had been the bass player. He played the double bass, but with the emergence of the electric bass which he felt unable to embrace, I found myself being the bass player in the church band. This was the case for a few years until younger bass players emerged and shared, and eventually took over the role altogether. A group of us formed a gospel band called Spiritual Rhythm, in which I was a co-lead singer with my cousin Gloria Brown.

Spiritual Rhythm rehearsed hard and enjoyed some success singing in churches, conventions, concert halls, even travelling to the United States to appear in our church's international assembly. Another highpoint of our time together was auditioning for Hughie Green's Opportunity Knocks. We thought we got through only to be told we missed the cut, just. We were gutted! Oh what might have been!

When another band was formed, some of us from Spiritual Rhythm became part of this new group while continuing to perform as Spiritual Rhythm. This alternative group made a LP titled, 'The Joyful Sound', in 1972, on which I contributed two tracks as lead singer as well as helped with backing singing on others. I particularly enjoyed the buzz of performing before large audiences in churches, places like Wembley Arena, Brighton Conference Centre, Digbeth Civic Hall, and Birmingham Town Hall among others. Those were exciting times.

My long-distance courting of Novelette continued apace. Not everybody was pleased. Before and back in the 1970s it had been common practice in our church not to be seen visibly courting. A Church of God of Prophecy 'Advice to Members' actually said, 'never form too close an intimacy with the opposite sex, as this can give the devil a foothold in your life'. I did not consider this to be bad advice, but it tended to act as an inhibiter on open expressions of fondness and love, even between married couples it seemed.

Living as we did a hundred miles apart, when we would meet at a convention, for example, we tended to sit together and as our relationship grew, we would hold hands. People began to notice and both of us were 'spoken to' by our respective pastors. We were individually warned to cool it, wait because we were too young for a serious relationship. There were justified concerns about two young people becoming romantically involved and without the means to marry. This type of scenario would have been witnessed before by our elders, often with predictable outcomes – pre-marital sex ending all too often with unprepared for pregnancy.

Our church tended to deal swiftly and decisively with such cases, disfellowshipping the offenders. Both Novelette and I were emerging young leaders, she in Children's Ministries in her London church, and I in teaching, singing, music, and possibly a future candidate for ministry. Little wonder then that our pastors and leaders were keen to nip this relationship in the bud.

I found that my spiritual fortunes took sudden twists and turns beyond my control. At one particular time when I was spiritually low I attended an annual district convention of my church in Birmingham. As befitting my mood, I sat in the nethermost corner of the auditorium, out of sight. Suddenly, over the loudspeaker came the voice of the convention moderator, Bishop Joseph N Powell, the District Overseer, 'Is Brother Aldred here? Come and sing us a song.' Stunned out of my spiritual and physical malaise I made my way to the platform and sang. This intervention had a tremendously revitalising effect on me way beyond the moment. From that day a bond developed between the Bishop and me and I would visit his home to spend time with him and his wife on several occasions when I visited London. Bishop Powell was a keen table tennis player and had a tennis table in his garage. Playing table tennis became a good background to some deep conversation about religion and politics.

My spiritual life tended to have its ups and downs. I had brought with me from Jamaica some unfinished business concerning being baptised with the Holy Spirit (I found that in England people tended to speak of the Holy Spirit in stead of the Holy Ghost), with the evidence of speaking in tongues, as required by my church. All the 'tarrying' in early morning prayer and revival meetings in Jamaica had failed to get me to the point of salvific acceptability; being saved, sanctified and filled. Having been in church all my life, baptised at eleven, and now just out of my teens, this was taking a very long time. Surely people must be wondering if I were living a double life? Why did God not see it fit to fill me with the Holy Spirit?

I was helping to teach a Sunday School class, singing solo and in groups, playing the bass in church, but still unable to get beyond the being 'saved'. Help was at hand in the form of a week of revival meetings under our new pastor. His daughter who had accompanied me to the works 'do' had become a good friend and told me in no uncertain terms that I needed to be filled with the Holy Spirit, or else! To emphasise the point she took off the tie I was wearing and told me I would not get it back until I was filled! This was becoming serious. Desperate. But how was I to accomplish that which had eluded me these years?

On the first night of the week of meetings, I dutifully went to the altar to 'tarry for the Holy Spirit', a regular act that had been unrewarded up to this point, apart from that once in Jamaica when I 'just missed it'. As the music band struck up and the singing of the song leaders and congregation got into full swing, I heard the distinctive voice of pastor's daughter in my ear, 'pray Joseph, pray'. Well, to this day I cannot explain what happened, but with those words it was as though I were transported into another realm, and lost myself into a spirituality that overwhelmed me as though unconscious. Next I knew I was being lifted from the floor with shouts of 'him fill, Joe fill'.

I have to admit to not knowing much about what happened, but whatever had happened I was a relieved, happy man. The theological talk about baptism with the Holy Spirit is that one is given power for service and to do miracles. But for me the issue was that no longer would I have to walk the walk of shame to the altar to tarry for the baptism of the Holy Spirit. I also got my tie back!

It lingers in my mind, to this day, that the momentous night of my spiritual experience followed the night before when a group of us young men stayed up all night 'chatting foolishness'. Scarcely could there have been a more inappropriate preparation for spiritual encounter and endowment with power. I muse that God has a sense of humour and a lesson to teach me about grace.

In the meantime I was taking every opportunity to visit Novelette at her North London home where she lived with her mum, father in law and siblings. Her mother seemed to like me and on occasions I would spend more time talking to her than I did to Novelette who almost always seemed to have household chores to do. On reflection, this could have been a tactic to keep her daughter away from me. I certainly got to know the main road to London, the M1, very well. Time came that I thought I wanted to introduce Novelette to my parents and we agreed a date. This was around the autumn of 1973 and I had not long turned twenty-one. The day arrived, but I received a call from Novelette saying her mother did not allow her to travel to Birmingham. I was so disappointed, devastated even. How could she?

It was in that state of youthful anger that I said to Novelette on the telephone, 'I think we should just get married'. I do not recall if she ever said 'yes'. Probably adopting the 'assumptive close' sales technique I learned from Mr Van Rees, I took it as read that the answer was 'yes'. I identified that Novelette's next birthday fell on a Saturday, the popular day for weddings in our church tradition, and we decided to get married on 10 August 1974. Novelette would be nineteen on that day and I would still be two months shy of my twenty-second birthday.

Eventually our wedding was announced and plans began in earnest to prepare for this ginormous step for both Novelette and I. Neither of us had saved up much and it was destined to be marrying on a shoestring. As time passed and our wedding day drew near life became something of a rollercoaster. It dawned that just maybe our ministers' counsel to wait had some wisdom. Neither Novelette at eighteen or I at twenty one had much by way of resources, financial or otherwise; and neither of our parents were able to help much with wedding costs – although both sides made sacrificial contributions. On Novelette's side, her mother and on my side my mother was very supportive.

Novelette was now making strenuous efforts to contact her biological father whom she had not seen since being a very little girl in Jamaica. Novelette is a love child whose young parents went their separate ways, father to the US and mother to England; both marrying others. Hence, Novelette has family from both her mother's and father's sides. We, but particularly she, would so love to have had her father walk her down the aisles. But Alas! It was not to be, although Novelette was to eventually find her dad in the US, only for him to pass away within months of meeting him and his three children, Novelette's siblings.

My father, Bra John was a different kettle of fish, as the saying goes. He made it clear to me that his contribution to me was my airfare from Jamaica to England in 1968, and as he was not happy with how I was conducting myself anyway, he had no further money to give me and may not even attend the wedding. Bra John did attend our wedding and gave a memorable speech punctuated with, 'Joseph, be a man'.

In my church tradition, marriage is a serious matter. Based on the bible, marriage is said to be an institution made by God and should not therefore be entered into lightly. Only after considerable prayer and fasting, and the wise counsel of spiritual leaders and parents should two people marry. However, in our case I had not spent much time in fasting and prayer before deciding Novelette was the woman I wanted to marry and settle down with for life. Our spiritual leaders felt we were too young to marry, and among our parents Bra John at least was not happy. Not exactly an encouraging start. And yet, as I write Novelette and I have just celebrated our ruby wedding anniversary!

I had been enchanted by Novelette's natural beauty, great personality and voice, and as the months passed, I became more and more confirmed in my view that she was the one for me. I describe my approach as faith on the move. In my mind I am a child of God and if my heavenly Father sees me travelling a path to destruction, I expect God to deliver me from evil (Matthew 6.13).

In the months leading up our wedding, Novelette and I used our monthly salaries to fund the increasing costs in a hand to mouth, shoestring kind of way. Somehow we managed, with help from both our matriarchal family leaders, our respective mothers. The wedding day came and my best man (now) Bishop Lenford Rowe ensured I got to the church on time. And so it was that on 10 August 1974 Novelette and I were married.

The venue was Novelette's local church, the Church of God of Prophecy, Tubbs Road, Harlesden, London; the officiating minister was Novelette's pastor, Bishop Lesmon Graham. My pastor, Bishop T A McCalla, played some part too. Much was said about these two young people, two little pickneys, marrying at such young ages, Novelette being nineteen on the day made for some poignancy.

It became clear that this marriage of two up and coming 'stars' in the church was advantageous to Bishop McCalla since Novelette would be leaving London to live in Birmingham and attend Bishop McCalla's church. I felt well supported with many of my family members attending, a full fifty two sweater coach with my Birmingham church friends travelled to London, the day capped by my beautiful young bride, Novelette Rose-Marie Smith, walking down the aisle to marry me!

Novelette and I were married without wedding rings. She did not wear any jewellery. If make-up was worn it was not ostentatious. Our church taught against the wearing of ornaments and even in a wedding ceremony rings were not exchanged. Jewellery were regarded as worldly. It took me a while to fully understand the roots of these teachings in Wesley's Holiness tradition that had become part of Pentecostal tenet.

Not every Pentecostal church was quite as strict as the Church of God of Prophecy, which seemed to perceive such pietistic prohibitions as consistent with its self-perception as 'The Church', God's peculiar people, a holy nation in the world. My church's exclusive nature, modified somewhat nowadays, was to become a real challenge to my theological understanding as time went by. But for now this was the institution that facilitated the joining together on my wife and I – wedding rings or not.

We were so short of funds that we asked the master of ceremonies at the reception that followed the wedding ceremony to collect an offering for us. By this means we had some pocket money on our honeymoon in Paris. We still had to walk almost everywhere. My father would have had little sympathy for us since he had questioned the idea of a honeymoon, feeling that we could just as well go straight home. Nor was this far from the advice my bank manager gave when prior to the wedding I applied for a loan to buy furniture for our flat. The Barclays Bank manager told me it might be best to acquire some second-hand furniture. I didn't get the bank loan, had hire purchase instead, and later wished I had paid more attention to the economic sense of that bank manager.

Paris was my first trip abroad since arriving from Jamaica and added to my growing sense of movement away from my Jamaican upbringing. And yet, it was more a building upon than a departure from those formative years that were still the major impression on who I thought myself to be.

I had experienced the most awful earache on the small twin engine plane flight to Paris, which rather disorientated me and could not have helped my tired and naive attempt at consummating our marriage on our first night together. My wife tells me too that I didn't even attempt to carry her over the threshold. Oh, boy! Not a terribly impressive start to married life.

Novelette and I returned from our week-long honeymoon stay in Paris and headed to her family home at Scrubs Lane in Harlesden. I expected a warm welcome to the newlyweds from her mum and family. I had missed one significant piece of detail and its effects. Novelette is her mum and dad's first child; and her mum was just out of her teens at Novelette's birth. The two of them had grown up together on the one hand sister-like, while on the other with Novelette taking on parental responsibilities for her younger siblings.

Though still a teenager, Novelette was also now working and contributing to the upkeep of the family home. So the prospects of her leaving home had far-reaching consequences I had not even thought about. These factors though, along with probably uncertainty for the future and safety of her daughter, seemed to have crystallised in Novelette's mum's mind and metamorphosed into a tumultuous outburst from her upon our arrival back from Paris. I did not understand it at the time, but knew it was serious. Novelette and I made a hasty exit with her relatively few belongings which all fitted into my car.

Prematurely, we were on our way to Birmingham and the flat we had agreed to rent as our first home. Driving up the M1 motorway for the first time with Novelette my wife in the front passenger seat was a dream come true. Each time when I had driven to London to visit her and left her at her mum's home I dreamed of the day when I would drive up the M1 going home with her in that seat. That dream had now become a reality. The two kids, with little money to our name, rented an apartment with few pieces of furniture all on Hire Purchase, were driving into the unknown to start the journey of making home and life together 'till death us do part'.

CHAPTER 3

From Marriage to Ministry 1974-1983

A month shy of six years since I came to England to join my parents, a fifteen year old country bumpkin from Top Mountain, St Catherine, Jamaica; unused to living in the developed western urban context, I was now a married man. Life had changed so fast that I was having trouble keeping up with myself. Our first home was a first floor flat that had been converted by the father of friends who were fellow members of the gospel group, 'The Joyful Sound'. It was in a large semi-detached house typical of the reasonably affluent area of Moseley, on the outskirts of Birmingham.

One of the few early promises I made to Novelette harped back to my training as an amateur tailor in Jamaica. I told her that I would always iron my own clothes because no one could iron better than I; and I have pretty much kept that promise apart from the odd occasion when due to lateness emergency help was required.

We had a large bedroom and lounge, our own kitchen/ diner, bathroom and toilet. We were fine there, but recall one indiscretion when Novelette and I must have been less than discreet with our, let's say, 'extended honeymoon activities' and our landlord who, with his wife slept in a room immediately below ours, knocked on our bedroom door to ask us to keep the noise down. Just a touch embarrassing was that!

It was not long after we were married that I lost my job as a copier salesman with APECO that went into liquidation. APECO had been slow to move from wet to dry toner and was losing its share of the copier market to those companies that tapped into the change. I had to return my company car, lost my monthly wage, and was thrown into turmoil with a new bride and bills to pay. I was quickly snapped up by another photocopier company Kale Infotec, an arch competitor of APECO, but unfortunately that did not last long.

Novelette, new to Birmingham, threw herself into finding a job, and soon did, so we had one income coming in although it was not enough. I was not used to being out of work and now married, this was a whole new world for me. At the same time Novelette and I were quickly settling down to married life and at church I was becoming more used in various capacities. I also began to undertake courses in church polity and ministry.

By the time I was in my mid-twenties, in addition to being Sunday School teacher, I was local Public Relations Director, Cell Group Leader and had been made Assistant Pastor. Church responsibilities came thick and fast and soon the training I was receiving felt inadequate for the tasks I was being charged with.

After losing my job with APECO and desperate for income, I decided to sign on at the Job Centre office. However, I found the process of signing on not to my liking, it felt degrading and I determined never to go back, but to make every effort to find a job. My meagre academic accomplishment to date did not qualify me for much in the world and my church, though deploying many of my skills, was not in the practice of employing anybody except the main pastor.

I trialled many things during this time, from education courses to commission only jobs selling from shoe laces to fire extinguishers to insurance.

Shortly after losing my company car, Novelette and I had scraped enough money together to purchase a second hand car which was not quite of the quality of my Ford Escort Estate that APECO provided, but it got us around. We drove it to our church convention in Brighton and had to be rescued by the emergency services! But we were young and innovative so found ways to move forward.

One fateful day as I searched for a suitable job, I responded to an advert for a salesman. I walked into the sales office of Anglian Windows in Dale End, Birmingham and was met by a small white man, smaller even than me, immaculately dressed. Peter Markham Randall was the branch manager. We had never met but as I walked through the door, with a big infectious smile, he said, 'Hello sambo!' For some reason, naivety or other, I was not offended as later I was told and came to believe I should have been.

Peter Markham Randall was from a generation of white English people for whom terms like 'sambo' was part of a colonial vocabulary, that did not necessarily indicate active racism towards the present 'victim' or 'object' of such language. Peter proceeded to ask me if I had ever sold double glazing before.

'No' I said.

'Never mind, come and work for me', he said, 'you can make lots of money. Let me show you the commission statements of some of my salesmen.'

He showed me some anonymous salesmen commission pay slips that were very impressive.

I told Peter I could not work on a commission only basis, as I had responsibilities as a newly married man. What's more, I told him I had got into debt since I lost my proper job. Peter asked me, 'How much do you owe?'

'About three hundred pounds', I said.

To my complete astonishment Peter reached up and took his chequebook from his jacket that hung on a nail on the wall. 'What's your name?'

I told him my name and he wrote a cheque for three hundred pounds, gave it to me and said, 'Pay your bills and come work for me. See you tomorrow.'

If Peter's opening remark was what I should expect from certain white people, his latter action completely blew me away, and taught me a salutary lesson – never judge a book by its cover and discern beyond words. I banked the cheque and started working for Peter Markham Randall, very successfully, becoming assistant branch manager and one of Anglian Window's star salesmen. Soon I earned enough to pay Peter back in full. I got a real buzz often being the only black salesman chasing an order from who usually were white home owners.

I have been in situations where I was in a white couple's house, having measured their windows for double-glazing at a cost of several thousands of pounds. They may or may not have seen other salesmen, usually they had and I was faced with the task of closing the deal, there and then. The maxim was that even with a red hot lead, all the well-meaning customer promises in the world, meant nothing once you left the house. This was always a cat and mouse game for high stakes: close the deal for thousands of pounds and I earn several hundred pounds commission, fail to close and I got nothing.

From start to finish, a sales situation was a game of cat and mouse, looking, asking, waiting to pounce, get agreement that buying and buying now was the best decision they could make. The salesman's task therefore was to make the case for a decision so the customer in saying 'yes', felt this was not only a good decision, but it was their decision, not one forced upon them by me. I achieved this peak, this mountain top experience many times in my sales career, both as a salesman and sales manager – but it's a high wire game of winner-takes-all.

I loved selling! It was never plain sailing being a salesman. I enjoyed periods of great success but periods of severe drought as well and mine turned out to be a career as a sales serial polygamist in that a bit like most football managers, irrespective of how much success you have, you know a sudden drought would mean you get the sack or are forced to move to greener pastures. I picked up the odd CCJ here and there as a consequence of being unable to maintain payments to creditors.

My wife suffered a series of miscarriages before we had our first daughter Marsha in 1977. Those were tough days. Somehow we survived. In many ways the mid-1970s to early 1980s were also brilliant, creative and progressive years. Following Marsha, my wife gave birth to Genelle and Alethea. My local church ministry matured confirming me in a series of roles from youth leader to Sunday School Superintendent, to Assistant Pastor.

Wider afield, I served my church as Regional Secretary for public relations and as temporary Pastor on three occasions in the Midlands, most conspicuously at the Coventry Church of

God of Prophecy. My singing career blossomed, both as a soloist and as part of the Spiritual Rhythms. And after moving from our first marital home in Rev'd Williams' Moseley home, and sharing a house with another young couple, Novelette and I moved into a council flat in Ladywood, Birmingham that felt more private and more suitable for our young daughters.

The Ladywood flat also provided a space where I counselled with emerging talent in the youth department; young men like Fabian Anderson who went on to become a minister of note in the Church of God of Prophecy. One topic that proved controversial was when I, as youth leader, raised with the young people in my church 'getting married young'. This provoked much debate and fallout that needed out of hours treatment and again our flat was a good venue for this kind of remedial ministry.

I was developing a reputation as someone who troubled waters. Nor was my reputation for radical thought and practice helped by a discussion I led on baptism in the Holy Spirit. In this I sought people's views on whether speaking in tongues was 'the' signifier that one had been baptised in the Spirit; even suggesting speaking in tongues can be cover for unholy lifestyles and maybe people should speak in tongues less and concentrate on more beneficial gifts like healing the sick and ministering to the poor. In one meeting a sister, much given to tongues speaking, became so enraged with the trajectory of the discussion that she picked up her bag, got up and walked out muttering, 'nobody not going to tek my Holy Ghost fram me'.

The early 1980s were maturing years for me. Becoming a father was very special. Having been present at the birth of our first daughter, I missed the birth of our second due to attendance at an international church conference but made sure I was at our third. My fathering in some regard has never in my view been much more than functional.

One question I have been asked repeatedly is, 'Do you not wish you had a son?' Hand on heart, I say and mean, 'No'. I do not conceive of the notion that a son is more valuable than a daughter and while I can see the desirability of the symmetry of a mixed-gendered brood, I have been happy to take what God gave. I would like to think I would have been equally happy with three boys. However, having daughters tended to mean much of the close up and personal stuff was left to Novelette who also had much more of a penchant for discipline that I could ever muster.

In later years, my daughters laughed at my attempts at discipline and punishment that rarely exceeded the odd slap and was based on bluff and bluster threats that they soon saw through. In fact, they seemed to view me as a bit of a weak link when seeking to get their way. Some of that was quite deliberate on my part because, although I grew up in a culture that saw corporal punishment as a necessary part of childhood discipline, I never got very much of it and shunned the idea even if I hadn't worked out how to discipline without resort to the belt. Threats and bribes sum up my approach. What I hope was clear to my children was that I loved them and wanted the very best for them. I felt proud as punch when our eldest told me at her wedding, 'Dad, you made us feel safe'.

In those days, my young family made several people feel safe. We provided shelter to friends and family members whose youngsters were struggling at home. Some came to stay with us for a while, some for quite a while. New people attending our church would invariably wind their way to us or we would find them and offer to take them home to Sunday lunch which sometimes led to more frequent visits.

One young lady, of Greek background, whose name I remember as Theognosia Yiasoumis Constantinou, was a regular visitor when our children were young. She introduced us to Greek food and I fell in love with the cuisine and discovered some wonderful Greek Restaurants, especially one in New Street, Birmingham. Finding her name a mouthful, I enquired early on in our friendship what to call her for short. 'Theognosia Yiasoumis Constantinou' she replied. Well, that told me! I was saddened to discover later through my ecumenical work that Theogonacia died in her mid-years.

One young lady who spent time with us on Sundays was a trainee teacher who went on to become a head teacher at an international school in Uganda. Others simply took breaks from challenging domestic situations until it was safe to return home. Still, with others, it was simply the development of human relationships in a religious community of mutuality. When we lived in Handsworth Wood in Birmingham, a neighbour befriended us. We soon discovered they were a cohabiting couple. Somehow Novelette and I had the maturity to befriend them unconditionally and have remained friends over the years. They eventually got married and the woman became a member of our local church.

I was not always aware of all the good we were doing at the time to a wide range of peoples, black, white, Asian and other; and in varying circumstances. It's been in later years that some have emerged from our past to remind us of what good we did way back when.

Money was sometimes short and the Child Benefit cash came in handy at times. Once whilst I worked as assistant manager for Singer Sewing Machine in Martineau Square in Birmingham City Centre, the pay was lousy even though the job had a veneer of respectability. I had some work done and I was experiencing some difficulty paying the odd job man who did the work for me. He resorted to stalking our flat in Ladywood to lay wait me to get his money. For several evenings, we played hide and seek as I would see his car near our flat and dillydallied until he ran out of patience and left. Those were awkward times.

Shortage of money had other consequences too; like my inability to maintain a car. In the dead of winter I was often taking our daughter to her child-minder who lived two miles away. During snow blizzards I would push the buggy whilst the elements beat me up with wind, rain, snow and cold taking their turn. Many were the times I longed for the heat of my native Jamaica.

Novelette and I learned the hard way to budget on a shoestring. I'd like to think those trying times, which were not all our times by any means, brought us closer together, bolstered our resolve to succeed together and to build a family together.

Some funny things happen in life. One fine morning whilst living in Ladywood I got all dressed up to go to work. I was trying my hand at selling insurance at the time. Suited and booted with briefcase in hand, I walked down the few flights of stairs from our flat and realised there was snow on the ground. Before I could decide whether to risk walking on the ice in my dressing shoes, or turn back to get some more appropriate snow boots, I had walked on to the snow and in a flash found myself flat on my back with the briefcase flung meters away as I desperately and involuntarily tried to protect myself. I quickly sat up in the snow, looked around wondering if anybody witnessed my indignity. I saw no one, so got up quickly, brushed myself off, picked up my briefcase and tried to recompose myself, before returning inside to my flat to get some shoes better equipped to walk on snow.

Also, whilst living in Ladywood I was challenged to support our daughter's nursery by learning to knit wool and taking part in a sponsored kitting competition. This I gladly did, raised some money for this worthy cause and found that a month or so later I could not even remember how to position the needles to knit.

Probably the funniest thing to happen though was the time I invited the national leader of a church whose teachings about Jesus I disagreed with. I telephoned him and told him I was interested in his church. He quickly arranged to meet me and we met at our flat. He diligently explained his church's 'Jesus Only' teachings and why Jehovah in the Old Testament was Jesus in the New; gave me a copy of his book on the subject and left. I learned much about his brand of faith but was less than honest in not being clear I only wanted some inside information on his faith. I had no intention of joining.

Along with other overzealous young men, I would also, from time to time, visit churches of this kind posing as though we were worshippers only to be able to pick doctrinal fights with the young people attending those churches. I could be quite Machiavellian really! I blame the mythical Bra Anancy I learned about in Jamaica.

My involvement with my beloved cricket grew during the early 1980s. Our local church cricket team was a very good one with several players who in other circumstances could have gone on to play for county and higher. We competed against myriad church and community teams, but our main and fiercest foe was another Church of God of Prophecy team, from Wolverhampton. This was given an edge because our pastor had previously been pastor at the Wolverhampton church and when he first arrived at ours he seemed to take every opportunity to compare us unfavourably with them.

So at every match between us we were determined to beat them badly and we generally got the better of Wolverhampton, with me playing a key role as opening bowler and No.6 batsman. We did well until one of them emerged who had trialled with a county team and we had the good fortune to not have to play against him for quite a while. Then one day he was available to play for the opposition and I ran in to bowl the first over to him as their opening batsman.

My first ball rapped him on the pad, plum in front of the stumps. We all appealed for LBW but the umpire turned down our appeal. From then onwards, he proceeded to knock me out of the attack and none of the other bowlers could cope with him either. By the time we got him out he had scored a hundred and we lost the match by quite a margin.

Having successfully undertaken all the training courses available from my local, national and international church, apart from the residential course available in the US, I was confirmed as my pastor's choice for assistant pastor in the Church of God of Prophecy's largest congregation in the UK, Aberdeen Street in Winson Green. Against all the odds, I was proving to be quite successful in a number of roles. This initially threatened to drive a wedge between my young colleagues and me, given our often vociferous criticisms of church leadership with which I was increasingly becoming identified.

I was seen by some of my peers as a kind of poacher turned gamekeeper. Bishop McCalla made it clear to the church that he had never before in his pastoral career appointed anyone as his assistant. That he now felt able to appoint me spoke eloquently about how he viewed me. It was difficult to understand why. As time went by, I realised he appreciated my method of doing things and handling situations in a forthright result focussed manner.

It may have helped to have had some discernible gifts as a speaker, organiser, administrator, and a way of effectively handling people. These gifts were oft called upon in my years as an assistant pastor. Just maybe Bishop McCalla found in me one of a few willing to stand up to him and yet remain loyal to him and the work of the local church. By the early 1980s the country bumpkin from Top Mountain, Jamaica had come a long way and although I was very much a salesman at heart, momentum was increasingly with my ministry in the church. As of then though, the church was not paying for my much utilised services.

From the late 1970s, the Cleveland USA international offices of the Church of God of Prophecy showed a marked interest in developing its work in Africa. I was asked to accompany my pastor to Kenya on a missionary trip to help with developing the fledgling work in that country in the name of the Church of God of Prophecy. The trip was led by a white American, Bishop Van Deventer and it appeared to me that it was a requirement that a white person had to lead even though we were going to an African country. This was my first visit to the continent of Africa and it was an exciting prospect.

We landed at Nairobi Airport and were put up in a hotel for a while before making our way to our destination, Kisumu. After falling asleep and waking at dusk, I looked out of the window and was alarmed to see many black heads of people walking outside – since leaving Jamaica as a boy I had not seen so many black people, apart from black congregations in church on a Sunday and at conventions. Later the same day, we picked up a car and, maybe because I was the youngest of the three, was asked to be the driver.

For several hours I drove from Nairobi, through Nkuru and on to Kisumu where we stayed in the Sunrise Hotel near Lake Victoria on the border with Uganda. During the challenging night drive on inadequate roads, the car suddenly dropped into a huge pothole, more a crater, which I saw but could not avoid. The bang was so loud I was sure a tyre had burst. I stopped the car and we all jumped out to look with a flashlight. Fortunately the tyre was intact and there was no discernible damage, and we continued on our way. The Sunrise Hotel in Kisumu provided the most wonderful food and I was pleased to be on African soil, the place of my ancestors.

During our three weeks in Kenya we preached, taught and visited missions. Everywhere we went there was a welcome party waiting. In spite of the lack of telephones in deep rural areas the people seemed to have highly developed communication systems and knew we were coming. Of great interest were our specially choreographed visits to the homes of some of the Kenyans. Unlike the great cooking at the Sunrise Hotel, that which we were treated to in homes left a little to be desired. The poor chicken on the plate reminded me of the small birds I used to shoot with my catapult as a boy in Jamaica, and generally the home cooking was somewhat unenticing to my Jamaican British taste buds.

We had been warned though to always eat what was offered or our hosts would be offended. I often tried and failed to get beyond a mouthful or two before giving up apologetically. This was made more challenging because there would inevitably be a couple of mother-figures standing close by encouraging me to eat. Overall though, my three weeks in Kenya was a real cultural reconnect with my African people and heritage.

I was amazed to see men holding hands as they walked along the streets; I was also amazed by the harmonic a Capella singing by what appeared to be spontaneously arranged community choirs. During this trip I learned something new. Bishop Van Deventer struggled even more that I did with the local food and on one occasion had a bit of an episode in the toilet we shared at our hotel room. As he eventually emerged from the toilet he asked urgently for matches.

We found some and he lit a match and took it into the toilet. This was the first I knew that a lit match can counter such smell. I also learned a few words of the local language of the Kisumu people, but they were quickly forgotten soon after we left for England, apart from the Swahili greeting, jambo.

Mum (Saana) and Dad (Bra John) in middle age. I thought they were really old. I am older now than they were then.

A young Joe in England

On our wedding day, with Mum (Saana), Dad (Bra John) and Great Uncle Isaac (far Left). 10 August 1974 London.

Radiant! Novelette, the love of my life.

With first daughter Marsha - isn't she cute?

Family time with daughters Marsha (back left), Genelle (back middle) Alethea (back right), me, granddaughter Arooj and Novelette

Fun time with Novelette

At the home where I was born, Top Mountain, St Catherine, Jamaica.

With my big sister Cynthia at the family home in Top Mountain, St Catherine, Jamaica.

Having a laugh with one of my brothers, Paul, at the family plot in Top Mountain, St Catherine, Jamaica.

Back at my old school in Paul Mountain, Jamaica with a former headmistress Mrs Madge Brown JP

Fried dumpling specialist! Making fried dumplings for sale for a cancer charity, in 2013

With my church cricket team of the 70s (back row, third from right is me)

With some of the 'lads' I grew up with (front row, far right is me)

A mission team with me in Ashford, Kent 1983.

In China with iconic pagoda in background, 1994

In China, with translator, 1994.

At my Master's Degree graduation, Sheffield University 1994.

At my Master's Degree graduation, 1994. (L-R) My sister Winsome, me, wife Novelette, daughter Genelle.

My family at our send-off, Sheffield 1996.
(L-R) Daughters: Marsha, Genelle, Alethea, Novelette and me.

Novelette and me at our send-off, Sheffield 1996.

With Novelette, my sister Gloria and her husband Doug

Proud recipient of my PhD Sheffield University, 2004

Proud recipient of my PhD, Sheffield University, 2004.
With Novelette, daughter Marsha and sister Gloria.

Getting excited while giving a lecture in 2012

My preach-teach pose

Meeting with Peers, MPs and black clergy at the House of Lords about Modern Slavery and Human Trafficking.

Novelette and me in Lagos, Nigeria. Guests at Redeemed Christian Church of God's Holy Ghost International Convention 2013.

Picking up an award for 'Man of Virtue'.

Outside No.10 Downing Street

At an inter-faith conference in Welwyn Garden City in 2014.
(Back far right is me)

At the Houses of Parliament in Jamaica, Novelette and me sampling the Speaker's Chair.

Book signing at launch of Thinking Outside the Box

The dinosaur and me at Disney

Novelette and me in Orlando with life-long friends as we marked our Ruby Wedding Anniversary, August 2014

Novelette and me on our Ruby wedding anniversary in Orlando, USA, 2014

Growing old gracefully.

CHAPTER 4

From Ashford, Oxford and Sheffield to Birmingham 1983-1996

I had been appointed a lay minister in a local Church Business Conference sometime during the late 1970s. In that meeting, without warning, Bishop McCalla called my name as one of a few individuals he had been observing and thought he had discerned the call of God upon our lives. He asked the local church to 'set us forth' as trial, or lay, ministers. In my Pentecostal tradition being 'set forth' is the beginning of a period of training and scrutiny leading to full ministerial credential, if the pastor and local church deemed the trial to have been successful; the candidate had little say in the matter. After two years I was deemed to have successfully completed my trial and was appointed a fully licensed minister of the Gospel in the Church of God of Prophecy.

There was no history of church ministry in my immediate family, though a great uncle was a pastor at the time. Among my friends, my call to ministry was something of a surprise. It was a total surprise to me at first, although gradually I had become used to the idea of a call to ministry of some sort. It became clear how seriously Bishop McCalla took me and my ministry when on one occasion I confided in him that I was in financial difficulty. His words are imprinted on my memory: 'Joseph, is the devil you know…is mash him want to mash up you ministry'. And with that he took me into his office, gave me what was a lot of money at the time, and told me to go pay my bills. From that day to this, we have never spoken about it.

Along with my nuclear family, my life was to change significantly in July 1983. I had been the area public relations officer, voluntary as all my church positions to date, for some years. And in recent times I had deputised for a pastor who had a stroke. These roles, added to other local ones meant my growing ministerial status had significantly increased.

The white American who was national overseer for the Church of God of Prophecy in England, Bishop Joe T White, had taken note of my progress and in a conversation with me informed me that he was aware of my contribution to my local church and although he was minded to appoint me to a church of my own, he wouldn't, at least not yet. His wish was that I stayed at Aberdeen Street Church and continued supporting Bishop McCalla.

We were a formidable team that had seen the church become easily the largest Church of God of Prophecy congregation in the United Kingdom. However, while keeping me at Aberdeen Street Church, Bishop White was minded to make me his national public relations officer at the coming national convention. I loved public relations and so this was music to my ears. Soon I received a letter confirming that at the national convention at Brighton Conference in July 1983, I would be appointed National Public Relations Officer for the Church of God of Prophecy in the United Kingdom and was invited to the national secretaries' breakfast on the Saturday morning of the convention.

Wow! The country boy had arrived on the national stage.

My church had become the spiritual and moral centre of my life. Growing up in the Church of God of Prophecy I had been taught that this alone was 'the Church of God'. The appropriate term for this position is 'exclusivity'. The Church of God of Prophecy was exclusively the church in the world. And so irrespective of what success one had outside of it, this was where life really mattered. Everything else was temporary but what was done for God through the church (of God of Prophecy) was eternal. Or so I believed.

As the 1983 national convention drew near, my family did our best to ensure we could pay our way to Brighton including travel, hotel, food and clothes. My wife and I went to Brighton that year with a spring in our steps, the children were too young to appreciate its significance, knowing that I would receive my first national appointment in the church. We duly attended the national secretaries' breakfast on Saturday and got a glimpse of the privileges that attended national officers and how the other half lived. I did not protest this special privilege, I embraced it.

Appointments were made during the last session of our national convention, after dinner on Sunday. As I waited patiently for time to pass, on Saturday night I was approached by my pastor requesting a chat with me. I thought nothing of it - we talked a lot when we were in our local church setting in Birmingham. However, this was to be different. What he told me was to drastically change the course of my ministry and life and that of my family for good. Apparently, the Regional Overseer for one of the smaller church districts had dropped a bombshell on the national administration. Without warning, he had advised them at the convention that he was emigrating to the United States and was flying out on Monday.

His plans were made and he was not continuing as Pastor and District Overseer for the Kent area. The national overseer and his close confidants, including my pastor who also served as a District Overseer, were faced with the daunting task of finding a replacement at short notice. The question he posed to me was, 'Are you willing to go?'

At that time, the national church had seven districts of which the Midlands, where I belonged, and London were premier. Nonetheless, smaller districts like Kent were important to the overall programme, and the national administration had reckoned that the current overseer was remaining in post and would have been re-appointed at the national convention. They could have chosen to leave the position vacant for a while but this was probably viewed as untidy. An organisation needs all its generals at their posts. Someone had to be found and found quickly!

This was the background to the conversation my pastor wanted to have with me. He said he had told the National Overseer that I could do the job. The National Overseer was thus minded to appoint me as the new District Overseer for District Seven and Pastor for three local churches. Usually one became an overseer only after extensive pastoral experience. I had little apart from brief deputising roles and having been assistant pastor for a few years. Yet my pastor had apparently told his colleagues, 'Joseph can do it'. This may have been a small district, but to put someone in there as Bishop without hands on pastoral experience was at best risky, at worst to court catastrophe.

I mulled this over with Novelette for a while on that Saturday night. I didn't even know where Kent was. We had two young children and Novelette was heavily pregnant with our third. It was an awkward time to up sticks. We had not long moved into a new home, one bought from the City Council, and were just coming to terms with the mortgage payments too. Maybe if we moved, things would improve as the church took care of us and gave us an opportunity to make a fresh start.

It required a great leap of faith to say, 'yes', but we felt 'yes' was the right answer. Our pastor had faith in us and we felt sure our best interests at heart. The National Overseer clearly also had faith in us and, even more importantly, I had been brought up to embrace the notion of being free from self-will. Translated, free from self-will meant whatever The Church asked you to do, no matter the personal cost, do it. Later that Saturday night I went to Bishop McCalla and told him we would go!

That decision had ramifications. Bishop McCalla's prized protégée was about to be taken away for Aberdeen Street and the dream team broken up. Considering the key positions I held, replacing me would require careful handling. Also, my appointment as National Public Relations Officer would not now go ahead. Ashford, where we would be based, was approximately two hundred miles from Birmingham, a distance one of my colleagues was to later suggest was so far away and so close to the sea that were it any further, the National Overseer would have had to give me a boat! So funny.

Sunday afternoon of the 1983 National Convention came and the National Overseer began to call the names of his appointees. District Seven was last to be called, and I suspect there were few in the five-thousand-seater Brighton Conference Centre who knew what was about to unfold as Bishop White read, 'District

Seven, District Overseer, Joseph Aldred'. The place erupted in a mixture of surprise and celebration.

I was thirty years old, my wife was twenty seven with two young girls and another one due to be born imminently. This was not an appointment many could have predicted. Some of my peers from Aberdeen Street Church streamed to the stage and hoisted me onto their shoulders for a few bounces. 'One of us' had been catapulted into the highest level of ministry our church had available.

It is thought the Church of God of Prophecy had not appointed anyone so young as a District Overseer before. This was a day to remember. In the height of the hubbub of excitement, one of the pastors who would be serving in my region whispered in my ear, 'Congratulations! If you need somewhere for you and your family to stay until you sort out your accommodation, I have a big house and you are all welcome to stay with my family'.

I did not know what to make of that magnanimous offer, but it was to come in very handy later. Out of the blue, I was to be on my way to become a District Overseer.

Before the convention at which I was unexpectedly appointed District Overseer, one evening there was a knock on my door. A group of three sisters from my church had come to visit me. They told me God had sent them to pray for me. They read some scripture texts, then asked for a basin and water, poured the water into the basin and washed my feet and dried them. Then they asked me to remove my shirt – I have to admit that at this stage I was becoming a little concerned.

Having removed my shirt they rubbed oil all over my body, head, hands, torso and feet. They then prayed and left. In retrospect that felt like the bible story of the woman who anointed Jesus' feet before his suffering and death. Just maybe this was a rite of passage to my sudden elevation to the office of Bishop. I am blessed with an equal degree of scepticism and pragmatism.

There was a gap between my appointment in July and taking office as District Overseer and Pastor in Kent in September. In these weeks, various arrangements had to be made to move our young family two hundred miles south. The church agreed to pay me a small stipend which would not be enough to live on so I would need to find other work, and we took up the pastor on his kind offer of temporary accommodation. I did not even visit the area before moving in what was to be another great adventure in this country boy's life.

My church held a send-off service for my family in which some flattering things were said about us. This was the first – possibly second, but I cannot recall if one was held for me when I left Jamaica in 1968 – of several send-offs we were to have in the years ahead. People at our local church who had watched and contributed to the fifteen-year evolution of the little boy who came from Top Mountain, Jamaica expressed real pride and joy in this development. The support of my local church for us as we stepped out in faith was assured, whatever that would mean we really did not know.

The time came when Novelette, our girls and I loaded our belongings into a removal van and off to Ashford we went.

Arriving in Ashford was quite a change for me. The black community was very small as was the church I had primary pastoral responsibility for. I had been used to being part of a large church of hundreds, the Ashford church was less than thirty, based on a few family clusters. On my first Sunday in Ashford the church gave me a very warm welcome as their new Pastor and District Overseer. At the close of the service everyone came forward to welcome me with a handshake and hug. All, except one.

I noticed that one sister never left her seat - she wasn't difficult to spot with the congregation being so small. Later when I enquired who she was and whether there was a reason why she didn't come forward to welcome me, the deacon informed me that the reason was that upon seeing me she asked if the church couldn't find a man to send to be their pastor, why did they have to send a boy! I was actually thirty years of age at the time. She at least was not impressed with the youthful looking, bright eyed, and bushy tailed new pastor. That was my first put down in Ashford, it would not be my last.

Ashford was one of three local churches I had responsibility for, as well as two other pastors. Unfortunately, my other two churches were even smaller than Ashford, to the point of being non-existent; the two pastors presided over similarly small congregations. Our family's living situation in our benevolent pastor's home was tight and we needed to look for alternative as soon as possible, which we did and after a few months found it.

I landed a part-time telesales job with a local foods supplier while Novelette settled down to motherhood and soon our third child arrived. I threw myself into my new role as District Overseer, including organising a district convention and a mission team that spent a week talking to people about faith in Christ.

After six months into my first year, I had scoped the task to which I had been sent and had serious doubts given the state of the churches in the district being so weak that I was not the right person to engage in the kind of evangelistic work needed to make a success of it. A key factor in my thinking was that my church was established among the black community in the main conurbations and Kent had a paucity of black people in its population.

It was in Kent in our new home that I suffered one of the most racist incidents. I was mowing my lawn when a small group of white young men approached me shouting 'nigger, nigger, nigger'.

I stood my ground and stared them out but I said not a word. They kept walking and I never saw them again. Generally, my experience in Kent was good and I got to understand that Ashford was a place for people having a second chance in life, usually second and third marriages. This did not augur well for a church that did not accept divorcees as members. And it was in trying to explain theological and doctrinal positions that I felt most out of my depth.

I realised that I had been quite protected in my previous incarnation in Birmingham in a church that exuded confidence and maybe even arrogance. Those who didn't agree with us could simply leave, whereas in Kent everything was smaller scale and one had to be more inclined to convince and nurture.

Although I organised and led a successful district convention and week-long mission team, some of whom met for the first time and were to remain friends for years to come, not everything was going well. I had to close the two churches that had other pastors on the grounds of dysfunctionality; and two of the three I had direct responsibility for also had to be closed on the same grounds. There were not the physical members to match the members on paper in all these cases.

There really was nothing to oversee. Only the church in Ashford remained, with me as pastor. I had not been ordained a Bishop and that was just as well because being ordained a Bishop for a non-existent district would have been a shambles. After deep discussions with my wife and much soul-searching, I made a decision that I would resign from being District Overseer and Pastor and return to Birmingham. Less than a year after the euphoria of my appointment, the hopes and expectations of my running a district had been reduced to very little. I had made my decision finally for the good of my family as I could not see how I would support them in the situation I was in.

I enjoyed and had fun in Kent too. For a start, Ashford was a much warmer place than Birmingham all year round, and I enjoyed that. It had a rural feel to it too and with rural Top Mountain, St Catherine, Jamaica only fifteen years in my memory, it was good to be somewhere that felt like country, not town or city.

I particularly enjoyed driving in the Kent countryside with its narrow and often winding roads. On a more personal note I was able to strike up quite a sporty relationship with the Deacon Douglas' children. We played badminton regularly at the local sports centre where I was able to renew my passion for a sport I was introduced to at Bourneville College and became quite a reasonable player at.

My wife and others from the church and community joined us from time to time. I found that as a spiritual leader I needed to show that I was interested in life beyond the church service and as I had long been somewhat worldly, I didn't find it difficult to don trainers, shorts and T-shirt and mix it with the young and young at heart on the badminton court.

My year in Ashford was eventful and signalled a decisive shift of career. I had some salutary experiences to take away with me into whatever lie ahead. One incident involving a minister's sexual immorality in my region led to me having to discipline him by recommending defrocking. That required some moral courage on my part, but was the right thing to do and I showed that when push came to shove I had what it took to not just threaten but act in the interest of the wellbeing of all concerned.

During the year I held a week's meeting and invited the founding overseer of the Church of God of Prophecy in England to preach. He had a healing ministry and we advertised the meetings as such. He, Herbert England, was white and his picture on promotional leaflets attracted some white attendees. A white woman was brought in a wheelchair and I met her at the door with a welcome. Clearly shocked to be greeted by a black minister, she enquired if this was the meeting with Bishop Herbert England. I told her it was and she agreed to be pushed inside our little worship centre. However, when she got in and looked around and saw the majority black attendance, she immediately demanded to be taken home.

For one of my two pastors I recommended not only the closedown of the church but that the pastor's young son who had shown some ministry promise be taken under the wings of another pastor in a viable church in the adjoining district. I am happy to say that young man has become a fully-fledged pastor in the Church of God of Prophecy today.

In the case of another minister who was involved in a fight with his partner, a serious case of abuse, I once had to physically restrain him, pinning him down on the ground in a headlock.

I met a white Christian brother once who told me he moved to Ashford after his marriage broke up. Prior to the breakup he was a staunch advocate of no divorce and if divorced, definitely no remarriage. He felt ashamed that he had changed his view and remarried, based solely on his personal circumstance. Yet again I met someone who because of his domestic situation was not a prospective member of my church. Since then, the Church of God of Prophecy has changed its position, now allowing marrying after divorce in certain circumstances.

So, the close of my year in Region 7 drew near and my exit plans were enacted. In agreement with the National Overseer I would hand over the pastoral responsibility of the Ashford church to Deacon Douglas, the only deacon in the church, and as his children provided the music and singing ministries, I felt he would be fine.

Unfortunately, Deacon Douglas' wife died suddenly during my year there and quite apart from the sadness that descended upon the Douglas family and members of our small church, I recall being in quite a quandary about what attire to wear for the funeral - the first one I would conduct as a fully-fledged Pastor.

There is nothing quite like a death to concentrate the mind. I had read somewhere that a minister did not have to wear black when officiating a funeral, but that grey is ok, and so with my nascent radical mind that was what I did. It did not seem to go down well with everyone in what was a conservative, traditional space. But I was determinedly making my mark, a trait that was destined to continue.

I had also recommended to the National Overseer that as the churches thought to be operating in Region 7 were not there, just Ashford, it made sense to merge this region with the London region. This was accepted and enacted as part of my exit strategy.

Having handed back our former Birmingham home to the City Council since it was acquired on a 100% mortgage basis and was in negative equity and having first been generously put up before acquiring a council flat in Ashford, I had now to seek accommodation in Birmingham once again to move to. Miraculously, we found someone willing to do an exchange through the respective councils with us, and we were able to move quite smoothly back to our home city. Other arrangements had to be made for the family, all of which were handled between my wife and myself.

The final part of the exit and resettlement strategy was employment. What would I do for work? My wife had these very young children and so bread winning rested squarely on my shoulders. I recall having this conversation with the National Overseer of the Church of God of Prophecy and he was keen to keep me in the 'employment' of the church. He seemed to understand fully my disappointment with having been posted two hundred miles away to oversee and pastor a virtually non-existent work and, my decision to leave. His suggestion was that I became the church's National Evangelist. Well, I'd never considered myself a professional evangelist, but thought I would have a go if the circumstances were amenable to mine.

For some time the National Overseer and I talked about this and agreed in principle. A sticking point though concerned pay. The overseer offered a kind of commission only, 'earn as you preach' terms. This seemed risky for a man with a young family, and there was more than an element of dislike for the terms on offer when I recalled that they were being offered to me by a white American overseer who was living in an all-expense paid parsonage, on a healthy salary. His risks were minimal but he was asking me to risk a lot in terms of financial stability.

He did manage to convince me, however, that if I followed a clear plan of regular revivals I could make a sufficient living from the fees/offerings from the churches I preached in. This worked to approximately fifty percent effectiveness, which was not satisfactory and yet again I found myself less than happy with my church appointment and leaning towards resignation at the end of the year with a view to go find a job that could support my family.

Returning to live in Birmingham in 1984, I was able to re-establish links with my local church in Winson Green, which felt a little surreal given just a year prior the same church had sent me off with great fanfare. I am surprised some didn't ask for their parting gifts back - some jokingly did. Alas! I was not much present at the church because as National Evangelist I would be away preaching on many Sundays and weekdays.

It was an eventful year, and the National Overseer had helpfully written to all local churches informing them of his appointment of me and encouraging them to call me to preach and to ensure I was remunerated properly. With all this and a favourable response, in fulfilling the role of National Evangelist, still I felt often like a square peg in a round hole. A lasting memory was one grateful wife whose husband had been a bit of a marriage rascal but who committed his life to Christ in a revival meeting I held.

Something in my preaching seemed to reach out to him. The immediate impact upon him was so dramatic she thought it nothing short of a miracle and bought me two lovely shirt and tie sets! Some were surprised at the nature of my preaching that year, because it was seemingly more animated in style. I just took it for granted that the Holy Spirit anointed me for the specific task, however inadequate I felt at times.

After returning from Kent to Birmingham in 1984, I discovered how challenging life can be. The excellent relationships I had enjoyed turned a little sour when I encountered behaviours at the Winson Green church involving some of my most cherished friends. I decided to approach one of them and explained why I felt compromised by what I had heard about before returning and was now seeing having returned.

The meeting did not go well and caused a breach in our friendship that was to affect us for some time. Such was my distaste for what was going on that I decided not to continue to worship at the church and moved instead to a nearby church of the same denomination.

Sometimes to protect your friends one has to make tough decisions at a high price. For me, it was better that I left that fellowship than remain there with some practices I disliked staring me in the face constantly with the potential consequence of my responding in a manner that would be unhelpful to all of us.

I realised that my tolerance level for inappropriateness is sometimes not very high, but at least I have learned to deal diplomatically even when acting precipitately and terminally because life has to go on. This is not to imply that I am some kind of puritan or saint.

As I approached the end of spring of 1985 and was actively contemplating my future as National Evangelist, I received an unexpected call. The Regional Bishop for the southeast district, Region Two, enquired if I would consider becoming the pastor of the Oxford Church. This would mean moving on from

National Evangelist after just one year, meaning back to back one-year stints at the national level of my church. I had arrived as a national officer but I wasn't sticking.

It's fair to say my first two years on the national scene had not set the world alight - two short appointments. At the time of Bishop Stone's offer to go to Oxford I was engaged by a sales company and was therefore not wholly available for the national evangelist post. Now almost a year since our return from Ashford, I had in fact just put down a deposit on a house for my family to move into. Bishop Stone's intervention brought about a significant shift including the prospect twice in two years of leaving Birmingham.

Oxford was tempting for a number of reasons. The pastor there at that time was a white American who had been brought in as part of a project to try to attract white people to the apparently anachronistic, overwhelmingly black, Church of God of Prophecy in Britain. I was interested to see what difference he had made to the ethnic profile of the Oxford Church and what I, steeped in Jamaican culture, could add.

My wife and I knew some of the members of the Oxford church and the prospect of being the spiritual leader for them was a tempting one. The most interesting prospect, however, was that one of the main leaders there hail from the same district in Jamaica as me. We had got baptised together as youngsters in the Top Mountain Church of God of Prophecy, St Catherine, Jamaica way back; and now there was a real prospect of us as adults reuniting to work together. My suffering wife and too young to understand children and I were soon to be on our way to Oxford to be pastor.

When we had moved, I received a telephone call from a member of the Church of God of Prophecy in Region Four from which I came. The caller was to the point, 'Bredda Aldred, me waan fe know is wha you do so why you caan stay inna Birmingham'.

Suffice it to say she was not pleased that I was again deployed outside of Birmingham! She was not alone. There was a view that there might have been a deliberate plan to send me 'to Coventry', banish me, because I was emerging as a free thinker, a loose cannon and too controversial for a conservative region like Region Four which covered the Midlands, and for historic reasons was the spiritual epicentre of the Church of God of Prophecy in Britain.

Before moving to Oxford I undertook some reconnaissance. The city had a small but not insignificant black population. The mostly young church numbered less than fifty, bigger than the Ashford congregation, but much smaller than my home church at Aberdeen Street. There was a sprinkling of white faces. They worshipped in the local Baptist church building in Cowley, meeting on Sunday afternoons after the Baptists had had their service. Nursery facilities for our children were good and things looked set fair.

We switched our potential house purchasing attention from Birmingham to Oxford but soon found that the terraced houses we thought we would not want to live in, we could not afford anyway. Quite a wakeup call that was. Our contacts helped us to secure a house for purchase in Whitney, Oxon, ten miles from the church but we simply could not afford to purchase anything in Oxford. The move went smoothly and I commenced my tenure as pastor on the first Sunday of September 1985. Commencing with my euphoric appointment in 1983, I was now in my third consecutive year as a national appointee in the Church of God of Prophecy; though now without the office of District Overseer or National Evangelist.

Oxford is well known for its excellent if elitist education system and although I was not there as a university student, it was to be a time of some real education and some profound growing up. Towards the end of my time in Birmingham before going to Kent, I was tangentially associated with a group of young men at the Aberdeen Street Church who were engaging with a university lecturer who had done studies on black churches in Britain, their histological and theological roots.

This engagement had had quite a disturbing impact on the local church's leadership and pitched the small group of my friends into deep antagonism with the local pastor. The battle raged during my year in Ashford and my year as National

Evangelist. And now into my third year, 'since leaving home' as it were, I had become more involved in discussions especially when on occasions my friends would visit me in Oxford. At issue were disputed doctrinal and historical teachings and beliefs tenaciously held by the Church of God of Prophecy.

The actual issues, such as the church's belief in exclusivity, the date of its origin, and other teachings rooted in its Holiness tradition about which the local leader was slavishly unrelenting, need not detain us here. Suffice it to say, the matter went as far as including the national overseer and I as a young pastor was beginning to take a keener and more affirming interest in the dissenting group's line of reasoning.

Maybe my juxtaposition to the Aberdeen Street church's leadership, as an assistant pastor and more, acted as deterrent while I was still there, but the landscape had changed significantly and there was bound to be trouble ahead.

I got stuck into my pastoral role in what was and became even more so a black majority but multicultural local church.

One major trauma during my Oxford time was an illness to my wife. She was diagnosed with a bone disorder and underwent a major operation on her hip that resulted in her being hospitalised for several weeks, then wheel chaired for six months, followed by being on crutches for a further six months. Ill-fated pregnancies apart, and they were tough enough, this was the most serious ailment to affect us as a couple since our marriage in 1974.

With the care of our three daughters, pastoring a church and making an additional living from sales, it was a stressful time. Add to this, my sister, who follows me in the Aldred family lineage, had a major nervous breakdown and needed much attention. Significantly, some of the pre-existent relationships I had expected to build on when in Oxford turned sour and did not materialise. My assumptions turned out to be precisely that, and I needed to work really hard at building new and in some ways rebuilding old relationships.

I learned you cannot recycle relationships, you have to build and maintain them. I found it disappointing that my assumptions were flawed. These and other challenges stretched me. But I was being stretched philosophically too.

One of the white families who attended the Oxford Church, stopped coming after a visit by the new National Overseer. During the visit, the Overseer was so pleased with what he saw that he suggested the congregation under my leadership was emerging as one of the most thriving and multiracial churches we had in the country. It was. In fact it was apparent that I, of African Caribbean descent, was having more success attracting whites and other nationalities than my white American predecessor!

But on the day of the National Overseer's visit, by which time we had relocated across the road from the Baptist church building we had been using to the local Anglican parish church, he parked his car in the church yard rather conspicuously. It was a significant sized car. Having noticed the absence of the white couple, I visited after a few weeks, only to be told they were not coming back because they hadn't realised our church was part of an American religious cult - and 'did you see the size of his car?'

On another note, a black attendee of our church, a man of no mean age, enthusiastically asked me for further information about the church. He told me that he had been attending churches for most of his life but had never found any he wanted to join, until now. He was so impressed with how we were doing church that he was interested in joining. I dutifully gave him my church's famed 'twenty nine teachings' leaflet to read. We met after a week or so and I asked if he'd thought any further about joining.

His reply was salutary and has stayed with me: 'Well, I can see all that you are against, what are you for?' He asked.

This led to a deep discussion that ended in him agreeing to become a member but his reservations about much of my church's official teachings and practices were evident. What was also evident to me was that the way in which I was doing church in Oxford was increasingly different from the official line.

Slowly I was being involved by the national and European leadership in training and mission opportunities, probably because I was beginning to emerge in meetings as a vociferous and forensic questioner of presenters. On one occasion, I took one of the international leaders aside at a European conference in Malta, and asked his advice about the gap I was discerning between official church teachings and my own thoughts and practices as a pastor.

I pointed out to him that, for example, if he were to walk into a Sunday service in my church in Oxford what he would see would not resemble a typical Church of God of Prophecy congregation. There were several worshippers wearing jewellery for instance, forbidden by the church, and I was not placing emphasis on teachings like compulsory tithing of income, becoming sanctified and baptised in the Holy Spirit evidenced by glossolalia since I believed the Holy Spirit is present in the life of every believer and glossolalia was not the only evidence of the Spirit's indwelling.

The international headquarters representative's response disappointed me. He simply asked, 'Why are you concerned about those things? There are many more matters in the bible to preach about'. I detected a green light to continue as I was going, but couldn't help contrasting that private advice with public affirmations for the church's teachings as laid down in statutes!

Oxford offered me a great space to experiment and develop in my faith and the art of being a pastor, stretching my congregation in various ways. But it wasn't all plain sailing! The church was built on the rock of a few families including the most significant family being that of the then district overseer who was pastor there before my immediate predecessor.

There were definitely times of turbulence as I developed the path I was taking as a leader. I wanted a much less doctrinally toxic church, less fixated on Pentecostal essentials and Church of God of Prophecy dogma, and more liberated to be disciples of Jesus Christ. I recall convening an emergency meeting to discuss what I felt was a silent but disturbing undercurrent of resistance by certain members of the congregation. They, to a man and woman, insisted and assured me they were supportive of me as pastor. I took their word at face value even though I felt sure resistance had been and continued to be present at the time. At least an opportunity to clear the air was useful for us all.

After two years living in Witney we took the plunge, sold up and in 1987 moved into Oxford, buying a house in the vicinity of the church in Cowley. This closer proximity to our worship centre became the catalyst for deeper involvement and engagement. It felt right that as leader I was living among my flock.

We did some creative things in Oxford, like took over the Town Hall for a Christmas play. Like deciding to scour the city for opportunities to volunteer, something that resulted in several individuals discovering volunteering and later professional vocations, in counselling for example, which was to impact on their lives for a long time. In moving into the Anglican Church in Cowley, my intention was to one day acquire it by transfer since it was not being used by the Anglicans, and the nature of the relationship I developed with the local Anglican leadership made that seem a highly likely possibility all the time I was in Oxford.

We had fun too, playing sports and meeting socially Sunday nights rather than holding services in church. I developed a great relationship with the 'mother of the church' in Oxford, Mrs Smith who was known to all as Miss Brown. In the most difficult of times, and there were more than a few, when I didn't want to burden my young wife with church affairs, I could drop in to Miss Brown and put my feet up, chat or be quiet. And there would almost inevitably be a meal coming soon after I'd arrived.

I took part in a charity twenty mile walk once and promptly convulsed on completion!

One of the funniest things that happened in Oxford, happened at a prayer meeting in the home of one of the white attendees. I had long had a weak spot for bad singing. I first noticed this when in Birmingham serving as assistant pastor with Bishop McCalla.

We visited a member's home and before we prayed and left the goodly sister decided to raise a song. As the song got going I could hear a voice that sounded so like a goat's bray and that tickled me. The short burst of the song with this discordant note ended and we, as was our custom, began to pray together. Every time I opened my mouth to pray, laughter blurted out. I tried, but failed, to control myself.

Well, in Oxford that night in this brother's house, this laughing gas returned. As we sang a song, I heard a similar 'goat's voice' and I found it impossible to control my laughter. This dear white fellow just could not sing but insisted on leading the song because the prayer meeting was in his house. It was a bad mistake on his part, but I was ashamed of myself as pastor laughing uncontrollably in, of all things, a prayer meeting!

One of the most sobering thing to happen to me in Oxford and which has haunted me for years was when a young man who had been incredibly industrious in the church before I arrived and since simply walked away without explanation. Still a teenager, he used to act as a caretaker, opening up the church for worship and ensuring the place was in a fit state for worship. He seemed a well-disposed young man, level headed, spiritual and mature beyond his years.

Then one Sunday morning he did as he had done on Sundays previously, opened up, prepared the hall for worship, and then as I walked into the church met me near the exit, handed me the keys and said he was off.

'Off where'? I asked.

'Off, leaving', he said.

This was inexplicable to me. He gave me no explanation. I was devastated. I can still only guess what may have been going on with him.

Probably the most profound development in Oxford though was a realisation I came to that the ministerial and theological training I had had up to that point was inadequate. I can't put a precise date on this epiphany, like all Kairos moments I suspect, development happens over time. I knew with increasing certainty that I was uncomfortable with some of my church's teachings and practices and disagreed with others. But I did not have the academic, intellectual and theological tools to handle my growing ill ease.

At one point I wrote the church's general headquarters in Cleveland, USA outlining in a three page letter my concerns about our teaching on 'against gold for ornament' that included even the banning of married people wearing wedding rings. About that time, a non-church attending husband of a female member did accost me one day in the street, telling me that since my church made his wife take off her ring, she must now be married to me! This was totemic of a wide range of concerns. I eventually got a reply from general headquarters encouraging me to pray that God's will be done.

This did not satisfy my ill ease. My conversations with my 'controversial' Birmingham friends continued and deepened. I was growing in my persuasion that because I was sometimes unable to articulate my differently orientated theological views, different from what I had been taught by my church on the nature of church, church history, glossolalia, tithes, sanctification, against wearing jewellery and makeup and more, I needed to do some serious study and reflection; the nature of which was not available within my church.

After making enquiries I enrolled on the certificate course in Old and New Testament Studies at St John's, an Anglican college in Nottingham. If I thought that my church suffered from shortcomings I was about to discover that I had many of my own as my early essays came back from marking, usually with a pass mark, but with a recurring markers' comments: where is the analysis? Where is the critique?

I was also experimenting with what I later came to know as ecumenism. The largely tenant/landlord relationship that had existed with the Baptist Church was strengthened even after we no longer rented their building for worship, and we were able to use it on some occasions. We had an emerging relationship with the Anglicans, whose building we now shared - although the one encounter I had with the Bishop of Oxford did not go terribly well since he was insistent that had his church treated the early Caribbean migrants well, churches like mine would not exist today. He was of course entitled to his view but that did not sit easy with me. I always had difficulties with the rationale that typecast black churches as merely the result of white rejection. I had a much more fruitful relationship with the team rector.

There were new churches emerging in Oxford, particularly African led ones with whom we were in primal conversation. A sister church, the New Testament Church of God, was also in Sheffield and their pastor and I enjoyed cordial relations. The main space for engaging in ecumenical relations was a Cowley Ministers Fraternal which I enjoyed very much.

Around 1988 an ecumenical event took place in Oxford that was to have a significant future consequence. The Centre for Black and White Christian Partnership, under the leadership of the Rt Rev'd Dr Patrick Kalilombe, a Catholic White Father and director of the Centre that was part of the Selly Oak Colleges in Birmingham, brought together a wide range of church leaders for dialogue and fellowship. This was different as its emphasis was on Christian relationship building between people of different cultures and ethnicities.

It was an interesting idea especially for a pastor with a growing ethnically diverse congregation. When I try to locate the genesis of my ecumenical interest, I think of this fortuitous moment in Oxford in the 1980s. This was to lead to other developments that added to my sense of where divine providence was leading.

Just as it seemed I was getting it together in Oxford, coming up to the end of my fourth year - a long time compared with my previous two postings both of which ended after one year - a new National Overseer, my contemporary Bishop Oswil 'Ossie' Williams, came to office and decided that my services were required elsewhere. I loved the grandeur of Oxford, and having not long relocated from Whitney into Oxford proper, I did not expect another move so soon.

The new overseer wanted me to take up a pastorate in Sheffield and become the District Overseer for that region, District Five, covering a very wide area, south to Derby and north as far as Scotland. Although I had served in the office of bishop as district overseer in Kent in 1983/4 I had not been ordained a bishop so was entering that office for the second time, now destined to be ordained a bishop in the Church of God of Prophecy. Reluctantly, my family and I were on the move again in September 1989, destination Sheffield.

This time my wife did the reconnaissance without me and returned enthusing over having met a handful of my prospective parishioners. One in particular had been so helpful that Novelette was quite won over. School for our girls was sorted very quickly and a deacon in the new church dealt in properties and was willing to loan us the use of a small house in Rotherham, near Sheffield, which we took him up on. I noted with some interest the kindness of people in this my third pastorate as in each case, help was forthcoming that made moving less of a chore than could have been the case otherwise. This says much about the code of benevolence that exists in the kingdom of God.

Arriving as pastor and area bishop in Sheffield in September 1989 I had to finally end my sales career as for the first time I was going to be in a full-time paid position in my church. I was still a relatively fresh faced thirty-seven years old, and therefore still a relatively young bishop elect and pastor, with a wife almost three years younger than I was and a young family of three daughters, two under ten years old. This was a larger congregation than Oxford's, though not large in the grand scheme of things, of just over one hundred members, with a wider community of friends.

Sheffield had benefitted from the pioneering community and pastoral work of Bishop Sigismund Caine who was its minister for over thirty years since he, with others, started that church among a growing Caribbean migrant community.

It had seen better days, however, and I was brought in to halt the decline that had set in. It's fair to say, my arrival was warmly welcome by all, in so far as I could tell, including even Bishop Caine's close friends who had his best interests at heart and recognised that his best years in that church were now behind him. It was time for a new start. For me, after two relatively short stints as pastor it was now time to settle down and build this congregation; as well as the wider District Five in Yorkshire and Scotland.

Apart from the enthusiastic welcome by the local church and district, an early introduction was initiated by the academic director of the Urban Theology Unit (UTU), Rev'd Dr John Vincent, a Methodist. A letter arrived soon after I had arrived in the city and before I had had chance to meet many people which read something like, 'Dear Joe. Welcome to Sheffield. I hear I should meet you to introduce you to UTU. Are you available on (say) Wednesday 25 October 1989? John'.

Thus began a relationship that was to have a profound, transformative effect on the course of my life and to which I will return below.

I had seen the place before, but arriving at the Church of God of Prophecy, Duke Street, Sheffield for the first Sunday in September to begin my pastorate was quite daunting.

Situated in the district of Parkhill next to sprawling council owned high rise flats, yet only a stone's throw from the city centre, the church property comprised an old Methodist chapel that had been added to over the years and an outside toilet. I arrived early on my first Sunday morning with my family but had to manhandle the old, broken wooden double gates to get my car on the driveway they led to. My initial thought was that there was a lot of repair work to do.

I was to discover that what I saw was the tip of an iceberg. It's not that nothing had been done, rather that the property was old and needed perennial repair, inside and outside. It turned out that one of the upstairs room where the ceiling was on the floor, had suffered a leak and was the subject of an insurance claim, but the repair was not done as other priorities were more demanding. Indeed, later research showed that the original property when purchased included three terraced houses that had been demolished. The entire place could have benefitted from a similar fate.

The sanctuary and everywhere needed an uplift and improving the quality of the physical space was to go hand in hand with improving the flagging morale of the community I had now come to lead.

The cumulated learning I had had from my previous two pastorates, in addition to my years observing Bishop McCalla as pastor in Birmingham, taught me that the pastor's relationship with leaders is of great significance if a church is to prosper. We agreed to meet monthly as a ministry team and quarterly as a wider leadership team, convening other meetings as and when necessary. I took on the bulk of the preaching but was very clear about the need to cultivate a sense of a team with the ministers and leaders I had inherited by providing regular if infrequent opportunities for those who could preach to do so.

None of the four deacons and three lay ministers I found had theological or ministry training apart from the basic in house denominational training that was the norm. I had not long completed my Old and New Testament studies at St John's and was myself theologically still a work in progress. What my new colleagues lacked in academic quality they made up for in enthusiasm and conscientiousness. I did not appoint an assistant in either of my previous pastorates, but here in Sheffield being pastor of a larger congregation than those two and with wider district overseer responsibility I made the decision to appoint one.

I appointed the only female in the ministerial team as my assistant pastor because, among other qualities, she possessed a sparky preaching style that complimented mine. Christine was a nursing professional and our joint task was to enable her to be comparably competent in theology and ministry as she was in her chosen profession. She soon started training in theology and ministry, in which she proved herself eminently capable; becoming a pastor in her own right in later years.

An early challenge was the role of treasurer. The treasurer I inherited was an amiable and generous spirited man, but had minimal bookkeeping experience and expertise. I knew I had to change him and bring in someone who had those skills or was capable of being trained. It was important, however, that I did not disrespect him. Not only was he a decent fellow, he had performed the role at the behest of my predecessor for several years. However, for the plans I had in mind someone who was or could be finance savvy was needed.

Praying for what wisdom God would give me, I spotted a replacement and decided to retire the treasurer. Over a period of about three months, I brought my intended new treasurer to serve alongside him as assistant and planned an appreciation service for the retiring treasurer. In that service, which took place within a normal church service, I presented him with a gold watch! The ministry team and I decided that this was a fitting tribute for someone who had done a job voluntarily for a very long time. I thoroughly enjoyed working with the team, and hoped they felt the same about working with me. I think they did.

As well as many positive aspects, there seemed to be quite a bit of indiscipline in the Sheffield congregation. Rumour had it that on occasions some members had come close to exchanging blows, even implicating the pastor as perpetrator or as victim, I was not sure and didn't want to ask. On one infamous occasion quite early in my tenure, there was an uproar in the adult Sunday School that always preceded the main Sunday service. One adult brother began to tear into the female superintendent, reprimanding her over one thing or another but being very personal and, in my view, highly disrespectful towards her.

I listened and watched for some seconds and decided that the matter had gone far enough, so, notwithstanding my newness, I stepped in, took the microphone and instructed that the Sunday School session was over! The superintendent who was under the cosh of the verbal assault was visibly relieved. I understood the need to be cautious in a new setting but I recognised bullying when I saw it. The following day I telephoned the offending brother and asked to see him. He agreed and I took one of the deacons with me. Once the pleasantries were over, I calmly asked him what the confrontation was about and he tried to explain.

I got the distinct impression that to him and some others this behaviour was not at all exceptional and that maybe I was overreacting. I may have been, but I told him that this kind of behaviour would not be tolerated in any church I pastor. Everybody would have to practice respect for each other. What's more, I told him that I took such a dim view of what happened on Sunday that if he ever did that or anything like it again, as Pastor I would convene an emergency members meeting and have him excommunicated on the spot for abusive behaviour. I had no idea if the church polity allowed for any such thing. But he got the message, so much so that he did not show up in church for a full six months after that meeting.

Some began to ask me what had happened to the brother, what had I done to him? I gathered he was a popular fellow and was a kind of warrior figure on the side of those he felt were being disadvantaged by the former pastor. He may have been testing my mettle as a new pastor, and if that was the case he certainly felt the force of my response. He never returned to church fully, but we had an interesting relationship from then on, during one meeting he told me that my small stature was deceiving and I seemed to have a steel fist inside my velvet-gloved hands.

Sheffield became fertile ground for me and my ministry. Organisationally and psychologically, it was far enough away from my denomination's conservative heartland of Birmingham and therefore lent itself to mine and other fertile minds, which led to ecclesiological innovations. It didn't take long for the people to 'get it' that their new pastor was liberal-minded and permissive. Apparently the church building had not used to being open much, apart for church services. I used it as my office from the start and let it be known, in addition to designating a particular day as my 'clinic' when, barring emergencies, people could come to see me and expect me to be there.

One young man who developed a keen interest in playing the drums saw an opportunity and approached me to ask if he could practice playing the drums while I was in the building. The clinic day was not suitable, so we agreed that other days were suitable. Well, the racket Chris made was sometimes overwhelming, especially when I had visitors to my office. Although the church hall, where the kit was kept, and my office were separated by a corridor and two solid walls, at times it were as though we were together in the same room. I allowed him to practice anyway, and he became an excellent drummer who didn't only play in church, but evolved into a professional drummer. Church can do a lot to encourage talent.

Back in the late 1980s and early 1990s micro computers were in their infancy. Instinctively I knew that my team of admin volunteers – which included Sonia who I am convinced is the fastest typist on planet earth – deserved to have a computer. So we daringly bought an IMB/Intel 286 computer! In today's terms it was not much more than a word processor, but it revolutionised the local church's admin and attitude. It seems everything could be done more quickly, from the monthly church reports, to finance records and reports and producing minutes; not to mention graphics!

One Sunday I noticed a young lady come to church with two little boys. When I enquired into her identity, I learnt that she was a single parent and had not long come from Jamaica and was keen to get along supporting herself and her two boys. The church's attitude to single mothers has not always been sympathetic and I had seen numerous occasions when young female church members who had become pregnant out of wedlock would be unceremoniously 'disfellowshipped' and 'turned over to the devil'.

I became increasingly convinced this was not the right or godly way to deal with people in vulnerable situations. Cynthia was a challenge and although I did not know how she came to be a single mum with two boys I wanted to help. Soon I discovered her ambition to go to university and that use of the church computer would be a major advantage since she could not afford a computer of her own. We allowed her to have virtually unlimited use of the IBM/Intel 286. She went on to get a BA Hons and to carve out an improved life path for her and her sons. I find that supporting someone instead of being judgemental is key to local church ministry to single parents.

I discovered that my open approach was becoming catalytic, giving permission for others to think about what they could do to improve ours and others' lives. We explored Black Theology, Black empowerment through discovering black people in the Bible. One mature female member suggested we start a luncheon club; and we pursued the idea making enquiries concerning what support we might get from the Sheffield Council. Initially the Council officials were less than welcoming, and with my new treasurer Pauline I had to fight the corner of our religious community to be considered part of the wider community.

One of my line of reasoning was simply that many members were tax payers and should not be excluded from grants because they belonged to a religious community that wished to provide food and entertainment in a space they found amenable because of their religious beliefs, especially when the group did not consider itself exclusive but welcomed anyone who wished to eat at the proposed luncheon club. We won the argument and received from the Council, grants to refurbish and equip the kitchen to semi-industrial standards plus ongoing revenue subsidies.

Sister Williams became the leader of the club but insisted that I attend not just the club but her team meetings. I sensed there was some degree of wariness there probably due to a historic atmosphere of adversarialism.

I loved to hear the joyful sound of dominoes being slammed on tables to the accompaniment of loud shouts of defiance or bluff as food and good company were consumed. The Sheffield Church had more than its fair share of domino players all of whom seemed capable of giving me, their pastor, six love; and often did. Sister Williams did a splendid job with the lunch club, and soon it went from one day to two days per week, eventually opening some week-ends and on bank holidays as well to feed the homeless left foodless by the closure of council-run provisions on bank holidays. In time, the homeless would be both fed and given a change of clothes donated by members on bank holidays.

A suggestion to start a coffee morning was pursued similarly, but with little success. We got started but the support was not good and we eventually decided to stop it. Sister Brown, its leader, was very disappointed but we had little choice. I learned that it was best to try new and support ideas but always with the clear understanding that if they didn't work, sentimentality must give way to common sense. This pragmatic approach – willing to initiate and just as willing to abandon – served me well.

I had not long arrived in Sheffield when I was tested as to my spirituality and moral mores. Two things stand out, and they were by no means the only challenges. My church, like many holiness churches, stressed on slender biblical authority that a Christian, more precisely, a church member must never marry a sinner, or more precisely, a non-church member.

My predecessor had refused to conduct a wedding between a member of the Sheffield church and her fiancé who, though not an atheist, was not a 'committed Christian' and not a member of the church. The common term used was, in the words of the King James Version of the bible, being 'unequally yoked', since light has no accord with darkness or righteousness with unrighteousness. So the question that awaited me was: 'Will you marry us, pastor'? And I felt like the whole church was watching and waiting to see how I would respond.

I was asked this directly in a meeting the couple requested. I thought about it, but not for long because I was clear in my mind that the church's interpretation of being unequally yoked was much too conservative. In the first place, an unbeliever in my mind was not the same as a non-church member.

For me, an unbeliever was an atheist, which declaredly this young man was not. Secondly, being unequally yoked with an unbeliever should not be aimed at marriage any more than it might be applied to other liaisons between a believer and an unbeliever, such as being in business together. There were things to discuss theologically and practically as you would in any pre-marriage counselling session, but nothing was insurmountable and so I said I would, and did, marry them.

Another similar, but less stressful challenge was a view held by some of the older brethren that young women should not wear trousers in the church, because they set a bad example to younger women about modesty in dress. I could not disagree more! Women in trousers had always seemed infinitely less risky and therefore more modest than skirts - we all remember the Marylyn Monroe picture of skirt raised exposing her underwear. In this instance too, I sided with a liberal understanding of how the Christian life should be lived. I had put down some key markers about the kind of pastor I was and the kind of church I wanted to build.

Sheffield continued to be a great place to innovate church praxis. We had regular concert style sessions at the local 'band stand' in the town Centre, where we would talk to people, share our faith in God and extend invites to our church services usually via leaflets prepared for these events. The responses were many and varied and whilst in retrospect we ought to have minded much more about the social realities of the people we met, the general responses suggested they loved the sense of uplift our music, singing and cheerfulness we brought for the two hours we spent on the band stand.

We took this open-air style of church to the new shopping Centre in Meadowhall, even taking a few of our regular Sunday services to the park at times, like Carnival. Other outreach initiatives saw us attempting to initiate prayer meetings in surrounding areas like Rotherham. Then there was a local Community Centre called SADDACA, the manager of which I got to know quite well as I deliberately lunched there on occasions, and visited whenever I could.

Eventually, I was asked by the Centre manager to conduct services at Easter and Christmas for users of the Centre. These became very popular. It is debatable what direct impact these external activities had on the local church but I was convinced a local church ought to be out and about in its community spreading cheer and something of the love of God for the world God created.

An urgent challenge that needed tackling was the refurbishment of our building. Members of the church and community, some of whom remembered the glory days of this church, were acutely aware of the extent of the degrading of the facilities. Even a relatively new addition to the property needed renovation. The corporate will was still there to raise the tone of the state of affairs but it appeared that the previous administration had run out of energy and the affairs of the local church left to whither on the vine.

Renewing the building therefore became totemic. If we refurbished the building we would ipso facto raise the morale of the people. I set about this with forensic gusto. We planned and launched a major assault on the dilapidated suite of buildings that included ripping out and replacing the pews with chairs in the main sanctuary; and landscaping the churchyard. Radically, I arranged with the local youth services to utilise the free labour of ex-convicts to do all the decorating. Not everybody was happy with ex-convicts on our property.

Local members putting their skills at our disposal, even though occasionally we had to pay, supplemented social services support. Apart from the splinter that lodged in my eye and for a while threatened my sight, two significant things happened as work got under way. First, a local businessman and friend of the church paid for the landscaping of the church yard, saying he was so impressed with what we were doing that he wanted to make a contribution. Second, a local craftsman, unknown to me at the time, said he wanted to make a lectern. The lectern turned out to be a substantial and sturdy mahogany wooden one that will last for many years to come.

I was overwhelmed by the generosity of members of the church and community. Time and again, I was reminded of the bible story of the rebuilding of the walls of Jerusalem in the Old Testament book of Nehemiah. It needed strong leadership, involvement of the people, and was not without opposition.

The Jerusalem wall required a lot of money and material. The restoration of the Duke Street church buildings and people was going to be no less demanding. The people I had come to were not as affluent as the ones I'd left behind in Oxford, although just as willing to spend and be spent for their beloved church. I could not complain about the way in which people stood with their new pastor. But it was equally clear that external funding would be needed to supplement the generosity of the congregation which needed to be maximised. With our new treasurer, Pauline, ministers and leaders I led in developing a four-part strategy.

First, to revolutionise the basis of giving from one of force, to voluntary committed giving. Second, we informed the national office that the local church had to cut back on how much money we paid to them and offered 10% of the total income. This left more cash in our local coffers. Third, I sought to discover how we could attract advertising funding for use of the walls outside the church for advertising. We didn't make millions but we made some money. Fourth, we aggressively sought to draw down funding from the local council, and though again they initially resisted we won the argument and received excellent support for our social projects. Undergirding all this was an unequivocal commitment that we would deliver on all the promises and targets for the money received. And I ensured we kept our word.

One of the highlights of the Duke Street church I pastored was its music and singing. black churches have a reputation for great Negro Spiritual, gospel music and singing. It is the case in Britain that many black church musicians and singers now ply their gifts wider in the secular music world. However, it is also true that this mark of musical excellence is by no means universal. So it is a source of rejoicing when you find yourself pastoring a congregation with excellent music and singing. Our church had adult and youth choirs, and soloists at our service on Sundays and on special occasions like concerts that made us proud.

There were some Sundays when the music and singing and corporate worship came together in ways that were simply glorious, heavenly, blissful and brought tears of joy to my eyes. I bragged that our worship leader, Gwen and her keyboard player husband Linval, were the best in the land, which may be stretching the truth a little, but only a little. Their reputation was such that when soul singer Michael Bolton did a concert in Sheffield, some of our singers were invited to be his backing group!

This did not go down well with the more conservative wing of the church, and again I had to stand firm to allow these talented young people to ply their gifts, this time for some pay, unlike the volunteerism implicit in singing and playing in the church. I just did not buy into the profane/holy dualism that seemed to dictate so much of church praxis. In this and other ways, I was determined to support the young people.

My support for our musicians and singings took various forms. At a time in the early 1990s when the use of overhead projectors was on the verge of becoming popular, replacing the church hymnal in favour of projecting the words of songs onto screens or walls, they were scarcely heard about in black Pentecostal churches. I decided my progressive church needed to have one. So I got whatever permission I needed from the treasurer and found a shop in Nottingham that sold them.

The journey felt like a real adventure into the unknown. I bought one, brought it back and there followed an exciting period of using this novel piece of equipment, creating a card filing system for retrieval of the films, and getting the congregation used to looking up instead of down at their hymn books. Worship leader Gwen handled it all with great wisdom. A second challenge was convincing the church to purchase the musical instruments used by the band, accompanied by a suite of microphones. The tradition was that musicians owned the musical instruments they played, with all of the cost implications of purchase and maintenance. The church enjoyed the benefit of their music without any of the attendant costs. It did not feel right.

We raised the funds needed and purchased all the amplifiers and instruments, including the keyboard and the drum kit. For once, some said, they could see where their money was going and for me this was a powerful statement of support for not only the musicians and singers but the entire local church. I wanted a church confident in its identity as a self-supporting people, not one in a colonial system raising funds to send off to headquarters as their main purpose for existing.

I discovered in Sheffield, if I had not learned it already, that no two people are alike. And in a congregation of well over a hundred people that difference can be quite sobering. I do not think I have ever desired to have docile and compliant members but my time in Ashford introduced me to the member who wouldn't join the welcoming party on my first Sunday there; in Oxford I realised that discord and disaffection can occur; and now in Sheffield I discovered that some members can be extremely challenging indeed.

At one moment of acute awkwardness in the Sheffield church, I resorted to chewing the cud with a new pastoral friend I had discovered through the fraternal I had come to know, a white man by the name of Peter Fenwick who led a white majority house church. Peter and I met on a semi regular basis of maybe once every two to three months, with him, an older man, playing the part of mentor, wise counsellor. So I put to Peter a particular challenge I was having with what I might call a small group of dissenters among the congregation.

There was a certain lack of congruence between these individuals and me, a kind of spiritual dissonance. Truth be known, I felt they thought I was not spiritual enough – not the first time that charge had been mooted in my short pastoral career. They may have had a point, who knows? I was suggesting to Peter a number of options I intended to deploy to win these people round. Peter in a stoic voice and posture reminded me of the Old Testament text that asks, 'can the Ethiopian change his skin or the leopard it's spots?'

I learned in that salutary moment not to spend valuable time trying to change the disposition of my opponents because we both were set in our ways and so long as no great offence was being caused, let sleeping dogs, leopards or Ethiopians lie. That was a significant lesson for me and one I was to remember for a very long time - some people, like former British Prime Minister Maggie Thatcher once said, are not for turning, so do not waste your time trying.

Dissonance was not the only challenging trait in the membership of the Sheffield church. On occasions, being a pastor placed me in the path of the predator member. One example will have to suffice. I was at home one evening when the telephone rang. The call was for me. When I got the phone, I immediately recognised the distinctive voice of the lady I had been told recently had let it be known that she was 'after' me. This was a strange call that began with an invitation to me to guess who it was on the phone. I refused to play along but that did little to stymie the flow of geniality that was forthcoming down the line.

The killer line went something like, 'Pastor, me all right you know...me healthy you know...me available you know...'

When I had had enough of the innuendos I interjected, 'Are you saying what I think you are saying, Sister X?'

To which the reply was, 'What you think I'm saying pastor?'

With that I brought the call to an end telling her, 'I do not know what kind of relationship you are expecting with your pastor, but I can tell you mine will be a purely spiritual one with you.'

And with that I hung up and never heard from her again. This did make for a rather awkward meeting the next time we met, but there was to be no further attempt to come after me, at least none that I noticed.

Sexual predators are very real in the church space and a pastor willing to play the field need not look far for opportunities. They range from the adoring and inviting eyes I have smiled knowingly and refusingly at, to the sister who met me as I descended the stage at a convention and told me bluntly and clearly that she had been lusting after me all day watching me sit on the stage with the other ministers. How does one respond to such blatancy? With the same knowing and refusing smile.

The relationship I struck up with Peter Fenwick, Pastor of the House Church, was symptomatic of way things developed, surprisingly. Indeed, that I was finding new white wayfarers and fellow travellers was a constant that I could trace back over a long time. From the double glazing sales manager who insulted me yet also lent me the money to get out of debt, to my time growing up at the Aberdeen Street church in Birmingham where whites were very much in a minority, yet a few of them attached themselves to the church and to my wife and I. In Ashford, Kent and in Oxford we had similar experiences.

The paradox continued in Sheffield. Key allies continue to be white in a country where racism is also very real. I found another ally in a white Assemblies of God minister, Pastor Jim McGeachie, a Scotsman pastoring in Rotherham, a town near Sheffield. At the time when we met, I was investigating resource material for new converts to Christianity. Pastor McGeachie generously showed me what he used. It was a twelve-lesson induction course that he had developed and was willing for me to use it. I wanted more though, and he agreed I could adapt it to my liking, which was what I did. In fact, the series was so successful that in addition to local use in my own church, some of my district bishop colleagues recommended it to churches in their areas and the take up was significant across the country.

But the relationships that emerged in Sheffield went beyond key white protagonists. Indeed the fraternal that developed was multicultural, black, white and other. There was the white Methodist minister, from whose church several black members practiced dual belonging, attending the Methodist church in the day and mine on Sunday nights. I was also able to strike up a deal to use the Methodist church building, significantly larger than Duke Street, for my regional conventions. Amazingly, not only was Rev'd Harrison willing to close their service down so we could use the building over the convention weekends, but we were given use for free! I ensured we gave them a good offering after each yearly use.

It was in Sheffield that I got a real taste for participating in pulpit swaps - not something I had participated in in previous pastorates in Ashford, Oxford, or indeed during my time as assistant pastor in Birmingham. Up to this time, as far as I can recall, all of my preaching had been done within my denomination. But in Sheffield, our multicultural fraternal flourished and I got opportunities to preach in several churches including Catholic, Anglican, Methodist, Baptist, United Reformed, New Testament Church of God and several black and white led independent evangelical and Pentecostal churches; Trinitarian and Oneness.

It gradually became clear though that not all of my black ministerial colleagues were as confident and relaxed in this mixed ecclesial economy as I and few others were. And the idea emerged that we needed a prior level of engagement, one that could nurture and build confidence in and among my black brother and sister ministers before some would be comfortable to hold their own in a multi-ethnic and multi denominational space. From this a black Pastors Fraternal was born. It did not replace the mixed one, it was meant to compliment and support it by building strong and confident black participation emboldened in the black space. I realised too that if this were to happen at all, it would be a slow and painful process.

I found that the diversity of black church traditions in Sheffield posed a real challenge and many opportunities for relationships too. So, the black leaders of the local Seventh

Day Adventist, of the New Testament Church of God, and of various brands of Oneness Pentecostal churches all became part of the fraternal. We had regular meetings together and apart. The formation of the Black Pastors Fraternal allowed us to address many of the social issues that affected the black community disproportionately yet indiscriminately of anyone's denominational allegiance.

The Black Pastors Fraternal functioned as long as I was willing to lead it. On more than one occasion, members forgot to turn up but would always respond positively to a telephone call reminder even when that was the same day and at the very time of the meeting from which they were now missing. Sadly, late arrival was part and parcel of how we operated. On one occasion, the Pastor who was to host a meeting, forgot about the meeting, causing us to stand outside his church until I phoned. The Pastor, who was at home, finally arrived offering his profuse apologies. I found that tolerance and a good sense of humour, buttressed by a steely determination not to allow the fraternal to collapse, worked wonders.

To a great extent, I was surprised how keen the black pastors were to be part of the Black Pastors Fraternal. Although it meant attending two fraternals for those of us who continued to attend the white-led one, this extra effort was more than compensated for by the alacrity with which my black peers warmed to this innovation. It seemed to me that diasporian life had made some of us suspicious of and uncomfortable around white-led constructs and white people, while at the same time pushed us towards ethnic-based affiliations that even overrode strong ecclesial and denominational belongings.

The concept of black space extended to the wider black community and it was not unusual to find some of us being called to bless new black businesses, or to accompany parents to their children's or grand children's schools as mediators and advocates.

I saw too how the few black run businesses and voluntary organisations I came across in Sheffield and elsewhere were often in trouble due, in large measure, to poor management and infighting, the source of which was more often than not competitive funding. It sometimes seemed to me that funding, even if funders did not set out to be deliberately divisive, ended up having that effect. This appeared to be the case whether organisations were successful or not in sourcing funding - the process encouraged a competitive dog eat dog environment that created an atmosphere of suspicion and non-cooperation. After all, why would you help to strengthen your potential opponents in the next funding round?

One of the most daring piece of work I, with others, attempted in Sheffield emerged from the Black Pastors Fraternal, which I unofficially led. We agreed to hold a major black-led citywide event in the Town Hall, open to all. A subgroup of the fraternal was set up with members drawn from across the black churches and covering all bases to make such an event happen. Nothing like this had been attempted before and none of us knew really what to expect.

In my own mind, I wanted us to hold a major event that would put on show the excellent organisation skills, music and singing talent and preaching of the black church. And I wanted to do this with white, Asian and other ethnic groups representing the cultural mix of Sheffield gathered together in one place. The planning group worked together for almost eighteen months of patient and meticulous planning to pull off 'Together in Unity' in the autumn of 1997. In fact, by the time it happened I had left Sheffield as pastor but continued to lead the planning group to completion.

We had some interesting challenges. Never before had Trinitarian Pentecostals, Oneness Pentecostals and Sabbatarians worked together on a corporate worship service. Many, including some pastors, believed it was neither possible nor desirable because it would water down what each believed and performed to the lowest common denominator. Our choice of preacher was particularly contentious. I was convinced, although I had not heard every black preacher in Sheffield, that the Seventh Day Church pastor, a young Rev'd Ian Sweeney, was the best preacher amongst us, and that if we are to profile the Black Church at its best we needed the most talented preacher to preach on our big night.

A feature of this project was that the planning group was made up mostly of younger people who had much more daring than the older denominationally hardened pastors and elders. And although some had misgivings; indeed we all had some misgivings at times, we shared a corporate sense of adventure, daring to go where no one had gone before and determined to overcome our fears and hang ups. Still, some pastors resisted the idea up to the last minute, and needed subtle arm-twisting by myself to give support. In the end I was not convinced that every black-led church closed that Sunday night.

When the day came, BBC Radio Sheffield ran the event as a lead news item. We had a hundred strong choir, a well-equipped music band, and people gathered from all quarters of the city and from much further afield. The Town Hall was packed. Any nervousness I felt through the day soon evaporated as people started pouring into the hall including local dignitaries like the Lord Mayor, other civic and religious leaders and politicians.

My deep desire to show off the local black Christian community working together and plying their religious skills, as a mark of excellence, was fulfilled beyond my wildest expectations. And the preacher for the night, Ian Sweeney excelled even his brilliant self with a sermon titled 'Skin-deep Christianity', echoing Dr Martin Luther King's message that human character should form the basis of value judgements about us over the colour of our skin. That he was Seventh Day Adventist was evidently lost even on those who had held reservations up to the end. 'Together in Unity' left an indelible impression on everyone in the Town Hall and beyond and is spoken about positively almost twenty years after.

Not all my ecumenical experiments worked to my advantage! There was a particular situation that ended disastrously. I had led my Sheffield congregation into supporting an evangelistic campaign by the local Seventh Day Adventist Church with a guest preacher from Jamaica. The two-weeks of meetings were held in a local park under a marquee. It was well-organised and demonstrated well the SDA's expertise in sponsoring tent meetings. On the first night of the meetings I was there with a significant number of my ministers, leaders and members in support of our fellow Christians from the SDA as together we reached out to the local community with the Gospel of Jesus.

All had gone well until the preacher came on to preach. With astonishing insensitivity, he proceeded to promote Adventism as the right way to be Christian and ridiculed every other church. His main venom was reserved for Pentecostals. For this preacher, Pentecostals were a laughing stock particularly because of their practice of 'speaking in tongues'. From his privileged position of the pulpit he seemed to have no sense of how hard we were working at inter-denominational cooperation and the extent to which these meetings were meant to be an expression of the Sheffield churches working together led, on this occasion, by the Adventists.

In one disingenuous sermon, he managed to undermine all the good work done previously. I was beyond embarrassment for the host Adventist pastor, as I was for having taken my people there to be so publically criticised without the right of reply. I pulled my church out of the collaboration that night, and told the local Adventist pastor, my friend, just how objectionable I found their guest preacher. Then to cap it all, after the two weeks were finished, a member from my congregation who had attended the tent meetings, a lapsed Adventist from Jamaica who had become a member of my church before my arrival, decided to re-join the Adventist church! I took it on the chin, put it all down to experience, but vowed not to allow this challenging experience to deter me from working ecumenically, but more wisely in future.

The most far-reaching aspect of my time in Sheffield was my academic studies, their outcomes and lasting impact on my life. As I have already alluded, my appetite for a higher level of theological study beyond that of the sub-degree denominational training I had received, had been whetted whilst pastoring in Oxford in the mid-1980s. Having arrived in Sheffield, I was soon greeted by an invitation to visit the Urban Theology Unit. This invitation was so innocuous and so unexpected, it was almost surreal. I do not generally regard myself as a highly spiritual-mystical person; I am more the spiritual-practical pragmatist.

I have not generally experienced God as overtly interventionist – I can think of only a handful of times in my life when God may have intervened directly. The overwhelming majority experience is of a God whose image, power and grace in me has enabled me to act often to bring about significant change. However, this approach by the Rev'd Dr John Vincent, coming out of the blue as it did inviting me to visit the UTU and coming from a white man who did not know me from Adam, warranted consideration for the label of divine intervention.

That John stayed with me as my supervisor through the entirety of my part-time masters and part-time PhD studies - a period approaching ten years - is remarkable beyond belief. Why would anybody do that for anybody? Why would a white man do that for a black man? All I can say is that he did it.

Engaging seriously in religious studies outside of my denomination changed my worldview significantly. Having for years had my religious education - some quite wholesome but some quasi, sometimes even pseudo - from my church, with the consequence of a mixture of under and miss-education, to be exposed to critical, liberal theological reflection was both challenging and liberating. This started in earnest with St John's Theological College in Nottingham and the Urban Theology Unit in Sheffield - with Sheffield University accreditation - was an even more creative learning space.

Although having had a history of providing ministry training and development for the Methodist Church, the director himself being Methodist, the UTU exerted no ideological hold on me as a student apart from permission to reflect and research deeply and that one's academic study followed the UTU action-reflection-action model. Having been invited by Dr Vincent to visit him at the UTU, I was soon enrolled on the Masters programme and decided to research my own local Church of God of Prophecy in Sheffield, it's history, beliefs and culture and future under the eventual thesis title, 'A Black-Majority Church's Future'.

My work involved setting up a research study group that assisted me in the research and reflective study in conjunction with my supervisors and tutors from the UTU and the University of Sheffield. Through this process we discovered some amazing things including the history of the building we worshipped in - that it belonged first to the Methodists, when it was built, how much it cost, who donated the money, and when and how the Church of God of Prophecy acquired it.

We discovered that the founding pastor, Bishop Caine went against the advice of the white, American-led national administration that advised him and his congregation not to purchase the buildings because they were in a state of dilapidation and would require expensive renovation and maintenance. Bishop Caine and the black congregation bought it anyway! My study involved an eventful series of engagements between young people and their elders in which both listened to each other; the elders telling their story of the journey that had brought them to where they were now, while the young shared their vision of the future in church and society.

These inter-generational conversations were riveting and highly educational for all of us. And there was a critical examination of the teachings of the Church of God of Prophecy in which the church did not get a good press. Once people got a chance to express themselves as opposed to having to give ascent, it was clear that members had many misgivings about the basis of faith and practices of the Church of God of Prophecy.

I was in a difficult place as pastor, feeling the need to be the upholder of the status quo but much more persuaded by the need to go on an exciting journey of critical discovery with my people and attempt to chart a different and better course. The process involved seemingly endless meetings, many late and some sleepless nights during which my wife and family, research team and local church were supportive beyond the call of duty.

The findings of the research project were written up in a 70,000 word thesis, which I defended at my viva voce and was awarded a distinction with the expressed encouragement of my examiners to push the study on towards a PhD. I was elated. My graduation followed in due course where I proudly donned my graduation gown and had a most wonderful time. What I did not know was that my family had arranged a celebration with many of our friends and those who had travelled with me on this amazing journey of theological, sociological, historical and spiritual discovery.

My wife Novelette had had the family home decorated with balloons and ribbons visible as I approached the house returning from the graduation ceremony at Sheffield University. I had not realised what this academic success, in which Novelette and the local church had participated, meant to them. It was as though all of us had been awarded this master's degree.

Buoyed by my master's success I was minded to follow the recommendation of my examiners to pursue a PhD but having exhausted my coffers during the previous two years of part time study I was not in a position to fund a PhD. When my elder sister Gloria, the sister immediately above me in our family lineage, heard about my dilemma, she generously offered to pay the fees for me. I will always be in her debt! At Sheffield University a PhD could be studied part time over eight years and the fees running into several thousands of pounds are paid for the first three, after which there is an annual continuing registration fee that I subsequently took care of.

I have reflected many times on my sister's generosity and thank God that such kind-heartedness existed in our family. I suspect that had Gloria not moved to the United States to practice her profession as a nurse there, having qualified in England, she might not have been financially able to help me in this way. It is great when mind and means come together; and I was the grateful beneficiary.

The Urban Theology Unit continued to be my study base for the PhD and Dr John Vincent continued to be my supervisor, with the accrediting University of Sheffield providing a second supervisor. The PhD was to occupy a total of eight and a half years and having started it whilst living and working in Sheffield completed it some years after my move to Birmingham in 1996. My second 70,000-word thesis, 'Respect: Understanding Caribbean British Christianity' was successfully defended and I was the proudest Jamaican country boy turned man in England on the planet at my graduation at Sheffield University. I was one of very few to be awarded a doctorate that day and we were greatly outnumbered by other degrees holders many of whom during the course of the pre and post-graduation festivities were keen to know why we few had on different and rare coloured gowns.

I took great delight in informing them that mine belonged to PhD graduates; what I heard in Jamaica, years later, described charmingly as the 'terminal degree'. It is fair to say that gaining a PhD transformed my life; for a start, I was determined, in the face of a little opposition from some not so well meaning people at the Baptist Church I was a co-pastor at the time, that I would put Dr before my name or PhD after it at every opportunity. The combination of Bishop and Dr in front of one's name has certainly made a difference to how many people interact with me. It is a little like money in the bank to start with which you then have to be careful how you spend it.

Studying for a PhD was the toughest and eventually the most satisfying thing I have done. From having always two supervisors – though from the university's side I got through four – with varying takes on what supervising a PhD candidate meant; to researching whilst working initially as Pastor and Regional Bishop; to searching for a research project and thesis that could make a contribution to the sum of theological knowledge; to the sheer hard slog of keep on keeping on to the finishing line: this was challenging. And yet nothing could beat the feeling of achievement when I collected the bound copies of my thesis from the University of Sheffield and that walk at graduation to collect the certificate.

In that moment I recalled my life story from a bare-foot country boy in Top Mountain, Jamaica attending Paul Mountain All-Age School to the man walking in a rare gown and cap in the salubrious hall of Sheffield University, England. During the eight and a half years of part-time study (I had successfully applied for a year's extension and completed half way through the ninth year), building on previous biblical studies at St John's College, particularly the three years of part-time study for my Master's, I had revolutionised my knowledge base.

As a result my Christianity became less biblio-dogmatic and more theological, less Eurocentric and more Caribbean/African centric, less other worldly and more this worldly, less church centric and more community centric. In sum, I believe I lost the 'tribal mark' of the Pentecostal tradition I had grown up in and became more Christian. Not everybody around me was or is pleased with the transformation.

Studying became a passion for my wife Novelette too. She had not done badly at school, left with several GCSEs but her domestic situation meant going to study A Levels and on to university was not even a fleeting consideration. She needed to find a job to help the family, and so she did. Now in Sheffield, once the children were of a certain age and less dependent, she grabbed the opportunity to study with both hands. Nov specialises in counselling and psychotherapy, going from certificate to diploma to a Master's Degree. It was the greatest of ironies when Novelette's MSc Certificate in Counselling and Psychotherapy and my PhD Certificate in Theology arrived through our letter box at the same time!

It has meant that the intellectual level of our relationship has grown over the years and I suspect, there are not that many homes that can boast a husband and wife with Master's and PhD – not unique by any means, but very special indeed. And this is felt not only at home in the quality of conversation and administrating domestic affairs; but in the manner in which we relate to church and matters of faith as well. If nothing else, education has caused both of us to become more demanding of what we expect from church in terms of sermon content for example, organisational structure and order. Our minds have been renewed.

My move from Oxford to Sheffield in 1989 saw me returning to the 'District Overseer' (sic) role I first occupied in 1983 when I was sent by my church to Kent. Six years older and wiser and although I had not asked for it, I was determined to make my mark as an Area Bishop, in addition to continuing to develop as a local pastor.

The churches I had in my region were few and far-flung. At one time, my region ranged from south in Derby, north to

Scotland and east to Manchester, and yet numbered less than fifteen local churches. I set about constructing a region that focussed on several things at once. Leadership and team building saw me meeting with my regional pastors and leaders monthly. I visited one local church each month too, and whilst visiting would preach and afterwards meet, often over a meal, with the local pastor, ministers and leaders.

I arranged, as was the national church custom, an annual area convention; but whereas this was traditionally held in one of our buildings, I initially move it to a large Methodist Church in Sheffield, and soon to the Octagon Centre that seated a thousand, even though my total membership was half that. My PR team would be extremely active at District Convention times inviting leaders and members of other churches, civic and community leaders, and determinedly pushing the boundaries of participation. I particularly encouraged young people to step up to the level of their God-given talents.

I encouraged our musicians and singers to be innovative and recall well the first time reggae was played in a convention. After the initial shock, people got to their feet and danced as their scepticism was overrun by cultural resonance! I was determined too that I would not advance or support Luddite tendencies in terms of dress codes. Over time, District Five emerged as a progressive region in the British Church of God of Prophecy.

With the appointment of the National Overseer who moved me from Oxford to Sheffield, I truly felt like my church had, at a stroke, become progressive. As a District Bishop, I operated as a member of the National Executive Council, attending monthly meetings that sought to provide leadership to the nation. I also served on various national church committees.

The Church of God of Prophecy in Britain has been overwhelmingly black, apart from a very short period after its inception in 1953 under the leadership of Herbert England, a white Englishman who established two white congregations in Bedford. That was before the arrival en-mass of Caribbean people. Since then, National Overseers had been white Americans until Bishop William's appointment in 1989. Suddenly a young black

British leader was at the helm raising in me hopes of a more culturally sensitive church and I felt culturally liberated.

Not only was Bishop Williams black British, he brought to the role years of management experience in the secular world in addition to pastoral experience. He was an intellectual and by that disposition gave licence to develop one's thinking about leadership and courage to apply the mind in discharging one's responsibilities. Alas! After just four years, Bishop Williams was re-deployed to the church's international headquarters in the United States. The suddenness of his departure left me and others wondering why. And it was widely rumoured that the old guard in the UK was unhappy about the nature and speed of change Bishop Williams was undertaking and called for his removal from office. A convenient solution for a bright and articulate person was apparent elevation to the international headquarters!

His replacement gave us a clue about his removal, as a conservative national overseer came in to the national office and quieted the wind of change some of us thought was blowing. Nevertheless, as a District Overseer, I tried to be as imaginative as possible in developing young people, in relaxing what I considered onerous church doctrinal stances on dress codes and social conduct, widening ecumenical relations, and encouraging a spirit of excellence in all areas.

A few anecdotes will help here to illustrate some of the challenges I experienced as district overseer. In a church that taught total abstinence against all liquor and strong drink, one on my district parishioners felt able to tell be that he never went to bed without downing a can of beer. What was a bishop to do about such insubordination to established church doctrine? I did nothing. This probably spoke volumes about my own lack of conviction concerning the veracity of this church teaching.

Then there was a moment that taught me much as one of my churches was engaged in a major new build project. At a meeting with the architects, national treasurer, local pastor and committee, it was mooted that the reason the architects had behaved shabbily was because we their clients were black people. The national treasurer was having none of that reasoning and instead made the observation that there were good and bad architects; and no architect worth their salt would deliver a poor build because of the ethnicity of their clients and risk damaging their reputation. This was regarded as wise words and steered the conversation towards a much more fruitful course dealing with the architects less as potential racists and much more as poor professionals. They quickly came onside and willingly addressed our concerns.

Then there was the rogue pastor who was a convicted child abuser that threw me almost completely because I never thought such crimes could ever be named among us: I was wrong! I found this relatively straightforward to deal with in that once the facts were known removal from office followed. And there were at least two occasions when I was called in to mediate in situations where a pastor was thought to have had their hands in the till. I found in each case that the pastor was actually given a raw deal, and did what they did out of need not greed. I instructed better treatment towards the pastors' financial needs and made clear that where a congregation is mean towards its servant, they cannot then become judges of moral character having been responsible for putting someone in harm's way in the first place. I realised that churches did not always take care of their pastors.

I travelled quite a lot during the time I served as District Overseer. I was asked by my international office to represent Headquarters at a national convention in Transkei, South Africa. Only later did I learn that this is the area in which the great Nelson Mandela was born. Attending that convention was quite an experience! This was my first international representative role and this was South Africa in the early 1990s preparing to extricate itself from apartheid. Transkei was under that system a country and I had the eerie experience of arriving at Johannesburg airport to be transferred onto an international flight to Transkei.

My first surprise was the care and attention with which the airport attendant looked after my transfer as for some reason there was a mix-up. She diligently sorted my travel to the denial of all who were behind me who had to be looked after by other attendants. I thought it strange to be treated so well in apartheid

South Africa. Eventually my transfer was sorted and I was directed to my plane. To my absolute surprise I was to fly on a single engine airplane on which I was the only passenger along with the two white pilots. More than once on the short flight that seemed to skim the earth all the way I wondered about what if these white guys threw me out of the little plane, whether I would ever be heard of again! I need not have worried as I arrived, safe and sound, in Transkei.

My intrigue with apartheid South Africa continued though as I landed at the tiny airport in Transkei. There on the tarmac, which doubled up as the airport lounge, to meet me was the manager of the hotel I had been booked into. He was white. He insisted on carrying my luggage to the car and once we had arrived at the hotel, to my room. This was not the treatment I expected and I learned afterwards that black visitors like me to South Africa was treated as honorary whites in contradistinction to how local blacks could expect to be treated.

It was all very counterintuitive and this good treatment marked my entire weeklong trip to South Africa/Transkei. Along with the visit I made to Kenya in the early 1980s, this was my second and last international church representative outing. There was little to report about the trip itself not least because the national convention to which I was sent and was due to happen over the weekend was over before I knew it. On the evening of the first day of arrival, after freshening up in the hotel, I was escorted by local church people to the convention venue where people worshipped vigorously for a very long time.

Eventually I was brought on to speak at what felt like after midnight. I spoke and spent quite a while afterwards fighting off sleep until I could fight no longer and asked if I could be taken to my hotel. My hosts kindly obliged and promised to return for me late morning to re-join the convention. When they eventually showed up around midday, they informed me the convention was over!

Apparently, they continued all night and finished the programme. Before I knew it, I was on my way back to England having spent the majority of my time in my hotel room. Not all my international travels on religious errands were as inglorious as the Transkei one. As a delegate, I attended conferences in several European countries and had fabulous times in Spain, Turkey, Germany and other countries. I even got the occasional opportunity to preach abroad.

Ever since the time in the 1980s when the Centre for Black and White Christian Partnership, under the directorship of Father Dr Patrick Kalilombe and the energetic administrative lead of Mavis Braham held their colourful multicultural ecumenical event in Oxford, I had wanted to visit the Centre in Birmingham. Now in the early 1990s I finally got and took the opportunity. The ever smiling Fr Kalilombe recognised me straight me straight away and began by telling me that he had thought of me just the day before and how providential it was that I now turned up at his Centre.

The reason he thought of me had to do with an exchange trip that was about to be made to China, arranged by the China desk at the ecumenical group Churches Together in Britain and Ireland – about which I had never heard. With few weeks to go the organisers had discovered they had no black person among their delegation. From our brief exchanges way back in the 1980s and probably from the odd reference by individuals he had wondered if I were available to join the group.

At first mention, it was the strangest of propositions, totally unexpected. I needed to go away and think and confer, not least with Novelette my wife. Seeing the Centre for Black and White Christian Partnership, in situ – a bungalow on the Selly Oak Colleges site – was strangely uplifting. I had had so little to do with it, yet as if a seed had been sown in Oxford back in the 1980s, it was as though I was in the company of friends in their lovely home. And to come away with the offer of an all-expenses paid trip to China to boot; well, this was some day!

I was in the middle of studying for my Master's degree with the Urban Theology Unit and Sheffield University at the time, and word was getting around that I was researching the black churches in Britain. A former, in fact founding director of the Centre for Black and White Christian Partnership, Dr Roswith

Gerloff, had done the seminal academic study on these churches. When I agreed to go to China, I found myself in the midst of theology, missiology and sociology academics of high calibre and I felt for the most part well out of my depth. We were in China for three weeks, went from city to city, and visited several universities, training institutes and churches.

Chinese cuisine tasted quite strange in China compared to in Britain and took some getting used to. But the scariest thing in China was my fear that each time we travelled by road I was about to witness people being run over by motor vehicles. It never happened, but I hadn't seen such risky driving in all my life – not even in Jamaica! This was China after their cultural revolution when religious institutions of all faiths considered to be 'foreign', like Christianity, were unceremoniously shut down. Now churches were being permitted to reopen but in strictly controlled and limited fashion. The Christians we met were intensely zealous about their faith in the face of their recent persecution and current state opposition.

But unlike the information I was given before leaving England that Christianity had to be underground, what I experienced was a vibrant open church, with packed churches everywhere we went on the three Sundays we were there, with loudspeakers blaring out of windows to cater for the many who couldn't get in.

I suspected that those churches that complied with government requirements to register with them were allowed to function, and those who refused on ideological grounds, largely under western influence and objection to communist restrictions, went underground. I reasoned that this was little different to what would happen in Britain were a church to refuse to register with the Charities Commission or Companies House. Inside the church services we attended the biggest cheer was reserved for the few words of Mandarin any of us had managed to learn. When we were out and about people often yelled: 'Poitier' after the famous actor Sidney Poitier, the one black man many Chinese seemed to know about. But something even more transformative happened whilst in China.

As we moved between places of theological and ministerial learning, I was often quizzed about how my church trained its ministers. The more the trip progressed, the more I was asked the question, the more embarrassed I became about the low level of training that was required to become a minister in my church tradition. I resorted eventually to tell of my own experience, untypical as it was, as one who did some training within my church, studied with St Johns College, and was now studying for my masters at Sheffield University. But deep down I knew I was being misleading and pledged that when I returned to England I would lobby my National Overseer and colleagues to put in place better arrangements for training of ministers.

I found myself pushing against an open door as the new National Overseer, Bishop Oswill Williams, was already thinking along those lines. Soon discussions were begun with St Johns College to offer its certificate studies to existing and trainee ministers in the Church of God of Prophecy, through its internal training organ, the Timothy School of Ministry. Not many people completed the course in the years that followed but I regarded this as a statement of intent; and further considered this as, at least in part, a fruit of my trip to China.

The chance trip to China did something else for me. It helped me develop a healthy regard for other faiths. Specifically, I met a Buddhist monk whilst there and engaged him in conversation. The young man was effectively on mission in a foreign country and culture, missing his family in Burma (I seem to recall, but am not sure) but was convinced he was doing God's will. I identified deeply with him in pursuing the will of God for one's life and found that although we came at this from different faith positions, there was a real sense of mutuality between us as we spoke.

It is impossible to say how impacting this was on me; one who had been brought up to believe that the only way to God is through Jesus. This encounter did not necessarily change my rhetoric but it certainly changed my boundaries of possibility, and as I am not charged with the keys to the Pearly Gates, I told myself that I had no need to make a judgement on the eternal destiny of the young devotee I had met thousands of miles from home. We were both foreigners and both men of faith. We did not exchange addresses and so I have no idea if he was similarly impacted as I was, and it does not matter.

The outcome of these providential encounters rests with the divine orchestrator of them. Since that trip to China, I have discovered an easy way with people who adhere to other faiths than Christianity.

In 1994 a few months short of her 72nd birthday my mother, Saana, passed away. Mother is almost exactly thirty years older than I and this has always held some kind of symbolism for me, though what precisely I am not sure. The circumstances of her death are sobering. Sometime before, our youngest sister Winsome and I travelled urgently to Jamaica because we heard that Saana was ill. She met us at the gate with a gleeful surprised look, asking 'what unnu doing here?' She was not expecting us. She had made a speedy recovery and we spent the ten days having fun and enjoying this unplanned holiday with our mum.

As we were about to leave Jamaica for England, Saana became emotional and said to us, 'This is the last time you are going to see me alive'.

'No Saana' we assured her.

She seemed to know something we did not. In the process of time, Novelette and I planned to take our three young daughters to Jamaica to see their grandmother and grandfather and to acquaint them with our motherland. We embarked on this well-telegraphed holiday, first spending time with Novelette's and my family in Miami.

Whilst there, we received news that Saana was unwell and had been hospitalised. We were due to fly to Jamaica in just a few days and so we hoped and prayed nothing would happen untoward before we got there. I contacted Rev'd Clinton Chisholm whom I had met in Sheffield as a fellow doctoral candidate and who had returned to Jamaica.

The circumstance of my meeting Clinton in Sheffield was funny. We had both arrived really early at a local barbershop. These barbershops have a reputation of being quite chaotic with no appointment system, so busy people try to arrive before anyone else so you can stake your claim to be first in the chair when the barber finally arrived, which could be a long way after the advertised opening time. In truth, a trip to a black barbershop can be a long visit, for which one need to set aside at least half a day.

As Clinton and I converged on the locked door, a good hour before opening time, one of us said 'I am here first you know bredda'. We both burst out laughing and continued talking when I discovered that he was in Sheffield from Jamaica studying. He had been a Baptist minister at the famous Phillippo Baptist Church in Spanish Town, but was on a long sabbatical. We became firm friends, as did our wives and children; and continued our contact via emails after his family returned to Jamaica.

From Miami I managed to get Clinton on the phone in Jamaica and explained to him the situation with my mother in Spanish Town Hospital. I asked that he might visit her for me, and he agreed. His reply was added to by a comment that was typical of the wit of the man: 'Spanish Town Hospital? Spanish Town Hospital is no place for sick people you know'. He duly visited mum and reported back by phone that he prayed for her and that her condition was very serious.

By this time, we were due in the Jamaica the following day. Landing at Kingston Airport we went straight to the hospital and immediately saw that Saana was 'travelling' as the Jamaicans say. She did not recognise or respond to me. This was s sobering experience. Death was imminent. Saana was on her way out short of her 72nd birthday. Too short by several years. By the time I arrived back at the hospital early the following day, the inevitable had happened; Saana had passed away during the night. I think of it now and I wonder why wasn't any of her children or husband at her bedside that night as she slipped into unconsciousness and passed from this life?

Saana had eleven of us and not one was there at her death: some of us were England, some in the US and just two of us on the island. I was saddened that Saana was already unconscious when I saw her and unaware of my presence. Migration in modern times, like life under slavery, separated families with devastating effects. Not nice!

When I arrived at Spanish Town Hospital the following morning and was told of Saana's passing, I asked to see her. What I witnessed has never left me and grieves me even as I type now. Her body was in what appeared as a makeshift morgue, and my mother was there half-naked almost indistinguishable from other bodies laid on top of each other. The smell of decomposing bodies was awful. Whatever refrigeration was in operation in that hot climate was at best ineffective if not inoperable.

I felt ashamed and angry. My mother deserved better, deserved to retain even a modicum of dignity in death. I made a speedy retreat and a semi-polite protest about the conditions at the hospital. I recalled Rev'd Chisholm's words that 'Spanish Town Hospital is no place for sick people'. It appeared this hospital was no place for dead people either.

There was something strangely ironic about the timing of Saana's death. Dying so soon after our arrival on the island for our family holiday, we did not need to either make a special journey or extend our stay to be at Saana's funeral. All my siblings, bar one, were on the island for the funeral. Strangely, this was a family renewal too, notwithstanding the sad circumstances, as from the United States and England we gathered. Three other matters were striking.

We had intended to stay at our family home on this holiday. However, as soon as our young daughters saw the house, and certainly after the first night, they made it clear they would not spend another night there. In fact, each of them took turns to keep watch for insects throughout the night. They were petrified of the mosquitos, lizards, and other creepy crawlies plentiful in a country home that was quite porous and did not benefit from air-conditioning. Interestingly, the house they saw had been extended quadrupling its original size that it was when I lived there as a child before travelling to England.

Telling them that made absolutely no difference – it was not the conditions they had been accustomed to in England. Rev'd Chisholm came to my aid as he agreed to have us stay at the manse he had vacated having resigned from the pastorate of Phillippo Baptist Church and moved out. We stayed there for the full two weeks and although it was not a five star hotel, it was much more spacious and it was in Spanish Town, not deep rural Top Mountain.

Second, when I visited the funeral directors to plan Saana's funeral, looking around the offices I was struck by the figurines of angelic beings – everyone including images of Jesus were of white European visage. It was evident to me that at this most crucial of life's passages my country was still in need of white reassurance. When I asked about this, the undertaker seemed oblivious to my reasoning and the questions that arose about colonial mind-sets.

But the most striking thing was my own reaction to Saana's death at her funeral. I cried like a baby and was incapable of making any contribution to the service. One of my sisters who consoled me on the day told me afterwards that although she was in mourning too, she felt sorry for me. I was quite traumatised at the thought, then the sight of my mother being put into the ground never to be seen again! Since 1994 Saana lives on in my heart.

It was probably sometime in 1995 when I requested a meeting with the National Overseer of the Church of God of Prophecy. It proved a pivotal one. I had been District Overseer for six years and had made various attempts to ameliorate the worst excesses of some of the church's teachings and advice to members that I found unhelpful, and in some cases oppressive. These included tithing as a requirement of membership and most certainly leadership, an absolute no to remarriage after divorce, total abstinence from all liquor and strong drink, non-wearing of jewellery, and various Americanisms like saluting a church flag clearly based on the American national flag system, and not swimming where men and women shared the same area.

Increasingly it became clear that whatever I tried to do in my territory would be overturned by articles written or sermons or edicts at National Conventions and the 'wagging fingers' of the self-appointed cadres of the 'old school'. This stymieing of spiritual character went, hand in hand, with the fact that the Church of God of Prophecy in the UK has never grown a church of any significant size in an age when megachurches was becoming a norm. Such conservative restrictive teachings had a stifling effect on spiritual and numerical growth, pandering to the death of the law rather than the life of grace.

In our meeting, I tried to explain to the Overseer that I believed the centre where he 'sat' needed to become a more dynamic influence for change and growth. Furthermore, the change of ethos and environment I and my colleagues in District Five were attempting to engender was constantly thwarted by a centre that made clear, in overt and covert ways, that it prefers toeing the party line on church teachings and practices and did not welcome theological and doctrinal innovations. I was always keen to point out that I am a firm believer in the idea of Holy Spirit empowerment, but not in those Pentecostal dogma that were rooted in poor hermeneutics.

I made clear my view that so long as we continued on the course we were, our church would never know dynamism and growth. Above all, I said I believed the British church needed to declare UDI from its American headquarters since enshrined in its constitution is the rule that doctrinal matters cannot be advanced by local or national churches, only by the General Assembly that had been convened for the entire one hundred years history of the Church's life in America each time. That fact has led essentially to an American church with franchises around the world whose only remit is to obey the edicts of the centre, many of which were created in an age of innocence by early church fathers that now, in the light of better understanding, needed reform. However, such reform would come only as and when and if it became expedient to the American agenda.

The meeting did not go well. We did not fall out but there was no meeting of minds. And I returned from that encounter with the National Overseer knowing deep in my heart that my time as an active Overseer and Pastor under the current administration and thinking was limited. I felt that my National Overseer was more interested in pleasing the American headquarters, not rocking the boat, than hearing the heart of one seeking progress. Indeed, I felt like a disloyal member or a bad boy who needed to get in line and stop making trouble. The Church was not about to change, and if at all, it would be excruciatingly slowly. I was keen to make progress in my ministry and life.

The unstoppable force had met the immovable object. It was a philosophical parting of the ways, though nothing changed for a while. My church as an institution and I were headed in two different directions. In the coming months, I was to lead my local church and district in new ways. Soon we renamed the church: the Duke Street Christian Centre separate from the adjoining Duke Street Community Centre, making it easier to seek funding for social projects.

One day after briefly discussing it with my leaders, I rid the church building of all the iconic '29 Prominent Bible Truths' booklets – I found them part of the problem of stunted growth; I recalled Brother Dash had asked me in Oxford, 'I can see what you are against, what are you for?' I relieved the church too of the church flag – there was to be no more flag saluting. And I decided that new members would not be required to take a 'covenant'. I wanted to lead a church that could breathe without the oppressive spirit imbued in these trappings of exclusivity.

A final piece of the liberating jigsaw, mentioned above, was a decision made by the church conference, led by me, to take charge of how much money to pay to the national headquarters. We decided on 10% of total income monthly; a significant reduction on what was being asked for by the governance rules. These actions did not mean Duke Street broke away from the Church of God of Prophecy, it was redefining its relationship.

As I got bolder, it was necessary to take not only my local church but my region with me. Some of my local officers were also my regional officers, so in some ways it was not difficult to find supporters of a more progressive way of being church. Neither was it not hard to find willing people in the region to encourage an ecumenical approach so we would always, at convention times, invite ministers and congregations to join us.

The model of increasing autonomy had to be tested further for roadworthiness. A key question though was the extent to which any of this was taking root in people's hearts and minds, not just in response to my prompting and leading. And it was at local church level that I found two examples of progress.

I had maintained that a consequence of the church attempting to enforce a legalistic tithing system was that, as with the taxman, once you have paid your dues, or practiced tax avoidance, no one goes looking for the taxman to give money voluntarily. And so it was rare to hear of a member leaving money in their will for our church. Equally, when a member received a windfall from redundancy, house sale or insurance claim, it was almost unheard of that they would tithe it. It is one thing tithing £100 at £10, it is quite another handing over £10,000 because you have had a windfall of £100,000!

But in that atmosphere of liberalising the church's teachings, one sister told me that she had left some money for the church in her will; and a brother came to see me in my vestry to tell me he had had a redundancy payment and while he might not have tithed it if that were his only option, he was making a substantial donation to the church from his gains. I was pleased by these acts of generosity bred, I believed, by a more liberating church administration, locally and regionally.

Something else happened too. I wrote a paper on 'committed generous giving' as a New Testament model for members' financial support of the church as one preferable to a dogmatic Old Testament tithing system. The paper was received by the then National Overseer who had it published as an article in the churches national rag, the Messenger of Truth.

I got lots of complimentary remarks from members from the more 'liberal' wing of the church and no discernible angst from anyone. Out of the blue, a letter arrived from General Headquarters in the US from the premier theologian of the church there, author of several books and church resource, Bishop Pruitt. He commended me for the article which he saw in the Messenger of Truth, and said how pleased he was to note this kind of thinking emerging in the church in England. He sought my permission and it was published in the church's international magazine, the White Wing Messenger.

However, I was brought down to earth a little while after when I noticed in a subsequent issue of the Messenger of Truth an article that was the opposite of mine, reminding the church of Malachi chapter 3, 'Shall a man rob God?'. I realised in that moment that not everybody was happy with my article and the line it took on a cardinal church teaching: tithing. Clearly, the National Overseer was brought to his senses by the legalistic wing of the church and someone was found to put the record straight. At the same time, there was little doubt that by encouraging committed freewill giving, my local church and region benefited greatly and as Pastor I was able to live off the proceeds of that committed giving as a full time pastor.

An early highlight of my time in Sheffield was being asked to be guest speaker at the launch of an organisation called the West Yorkshire African Caribbean Council of Churches (WYACCC). It was a dark and dismal evening in Yorkshire, the sort of winter's night I was to become quite used to; damp and dark from early evening. I got all spruced up and ready to go and deliver my talk about the history of racism and enslavement that had brought people, like the majority of my listeners, to Britain as economic migrants, only to continue to face persistent racism. Of how the black churches were enterprising yet divided, had provided a social and spiritual home for migrants but were now facing a question of relevance for younger generations; praising the like of Dr Roswith Gerloff for their work of researching and analysing the black Church in Britain as a phenomenon yet needing now black researchers and analysts and theologians; and such like. My talk was warmly, sometimes rapturously, received. Yet, two outcomes from that night were to surprise me greatly.

Immediately I had finished speaking, a white woman, one of the few in the audience that night, made a beeline for me. Smiling broadly, she reached out for my hand and in a thick German accent said, 'hello, I'm Roswith Gerloff'. I was rendered almost speechless! Never in my wildest dreams had I presumed that this renowned researcher of the Black Church Movement, whose work I had been citing generously, attributed thankfully, would be in a meeting in West Yorkshire on a gloomy winter's evening listening to me. You just never know who is going to turn up where.

The other surprising thing that emerged from my talk that evening was that several years later, now working for Churches Together in England, a colleague informed me that he and his wife were at that meeting I addressed those years before. Upon hearing my talk, his wife said to him, on their way home that night, 'that man is racist'. I never knowingly met them that night, but again who was to know that we would meet up later as members of staff of the same organisation! He didn't say whether his wife had changed her mind about me, but I put that down to the shock some white people may have when they hear a recounting of some of the racist and colonialist past of Europe, especially by a confident and assertive black person.

Those who know me well, know that I do not whiten all white people with the same brush. I do believe that Europe has a corporate sin of which to repent when it comes to its treatment of people of African descent – other people groups can speak for themselves – that of the sin of mass enslavement, dehumanisation and disrespect of Black Africans. In this regard, reparations are still required. My reason for mentioning this here is to emphasise that at key moments in my life in England, invariably a white person has either been catalytic or has been there. Two instances will suffice.

As my interest in matters wider than my denomination intensified, mainly driven by my university research into the sociology and theology of the Black Church Movement in Britain and what I saw as rampant fragmentation that needed addressing, I was invited by a media council, the precise name of which escapes me. I used to travel from Sheffield to London to these meetings quarterly.

On one such occasion, after I had participated in a meeting having played my part fully as I always tried to do – Sheffield to London return is a major commitment and I always felt I had a duty to participate fully to justify making the round trip – a white woman, who I later learned was a BBC executive, approached me and asked who I was and where I was from. I told her. She then said, 'You have a lovely voice for radio'. She proceeded to ask my permission to circulate my contact details within the BBC as someone who could speak to socio-cultural-spiritual matters to do with the black church and community. Thereby started a part-time career in broadcasting that continues to this day!

A second intervention was by the aforementioned Roswith Gerloff. Although we had not had a lot of dealings, we had a key one when the World Council of Churches (WCC) decided to convene a consultation with Black Churches in Britain. It was held in Leeds on the 30th of November to the 2nd December 1995, as part of the WCC's consultation process with Pentecostals around the world. I had written a challenging summary of the event which did not go down well with some including Roswith. She may have found my summing up of the WCC conference problematic but I suspect my forthrightness made its mark.

Not only did I find myself being invited to WCC linked conferences and initiatives abroad, but it was Roswith herself who, in early 1996, alerted me to an opportunity that was to significantly impact on my life. Although I had visited the Centre for Black and White Christian Partnership in Birmingham and had met its Director, Father Dr Patrick Kalilumbe again years after first meeting him in Oxford, and had gone on the educational exchange trip to China; I was unaware that the post of director was about to be advertised: Patrick was about to move on. Roswith encouraged, nay, told me to apply. I did apply and got the job, but it was not straightforward.

This was a challenging time for me, my family, local church and the district I was bishop for. Undoubtedly, I was unsettled but ministry and life in general on all fronts was going well as were my studies. I had successfully defended my Masters viva voce and earned distinction with strong recommendation from my examiners that I now push on to do a PhD; and to add to my dilemma, another job had emerged for the Director of the African and Caribbean Evangelical Alliance.

My contacts there, many friends among them, were keen for me to consider that post too. Suddenly two great opportunities presented themselves to exit ministry in my denomination; but to walk away from a pastorate and a bishop's see was a daunting prospect, as was the possibility of moving the family home again. Philosophically, I warmed more to the Centre for Black and White Christian Partnership position. The African and Caribbean Evangelical Alliance one felt strangely restrictive mainly because of its close affiliation with its parent organisation the Evangelical Alliance.

Even back then I instinctively knew that although I regarded myself as an evangelical Christian, mine had a small 'e'. While I faced and reasoned these dilemmas, neither job was a surety. After discussions with my wife Novelette, I resolved that I would hedge my bets and apply for both jobs and see which way the wind was blowing or the Lord was leading.

The Centre for Black and White Christian Partnership post was advertised before the African and Caribbean Evangelical Alliance one and I applied for it. I was invited to interview! On the day of the interview, I arrived at the grounds of Selly Oak Colleges and as I looked for a parking space there in a car waiting was a friend of mine who was also being interviewed for the post. I had no idea and as we had met at the WCC conference in Leeds it was eerie that here we were again. It did not feel good. I think I waved to him but did not approach his car and carried on trying to manage my own nervousness.

The interview seemed to go well but it was not possible to tell how successful I had been in convincing the panel I was the right man for the job of leading this prestigious and ground-breaking project forward. I later learned that they were minded to appoint someone from a Caribbean background and to that degree, I fitted the bill more so than my friend who was from an African background. I do not know who else, if anybody, was interviewed. But later that evening whilst staying at the national parsonage and home of the National Overseer, who was aware that I was up to something but did not know the full possible implications, the telephone call came from the interview panel chair to congratulate me and offer me the job. I accepted without hesitation. I was elated. My National Overseer was less so, especially when I told him I intended to step down from being Pastor and Area Bishop.

I telephoned my wife and we were reservedly happy as I was at the parsonage of a slightly puzzled National Overseer, who I had not previously brought up to speed with the consequences of my being a successful job applicant and for good reasons too as I had no way of knowing whether I would have been offered the job.

Interestingly, the post at the African and Caribbean Evangelical Alliance had still not been advertised at this point and ironically, I ended up serving as one of the members of the Interviewing Panel for the post a few months later. One of my fellow panel members at that interview made the remark, when we were less than overwhelmed about the quality of most of the candidates, 'The problem is that the person who should be on that side of the table is on this side'. I understood well what was implied. I felt though that I was in the right place, a more liberal space - as Director of the Centre for Black and White Christian Partnership, than the more conservative evangelical space that would be the African and Caribbean Evangelical Alliance.

The news that I would be leaving my pastorate and District Overseer's see did not go down well with my leaders and members. Particularly at Duke Street, it did not go down well. In a meeting when I broke the news to the local church, one brother pointedly reminded me that I had said not so long ago that I had no intention to move on. How quickly intentions can change. I am sure I meant it at the time I said it, but now circumstances had changed. Even those few who belonged to the 'awkward squad' – the leopard that will never change its spots - found the time to beat a path to me over the weeks afterwards to tell me how much they appreciated my ministry and that of my wife and family and their regret at our decision to leave. I jokingly responded to one, 'But it's in part because of you why I'm leaving'; the joke fell flat.

I discovered that one is never as popular as when one is about to leave a place. My family and I had a splendid seven years (1989-1996) in Sheffield pastoring and ministering as Bishop. Overwhelmingly people treated us well, and I hope the overwhelming majority felt we had done the same; that certainly was my intention and resolve. We had opportunity in two farewell services, one local and one district wide, to express gratitude and listen to people's expressions of love and appreciation. They were years of innovation and change for the church, region, family and me. I loved every minute of it.

But the time went by quickly and when it come the end of August 1996, my family were on our way to Birmingham, again, and for the first time in more than a decade I was to be outside the employ of my church organisation. A new world was about to open up!

CHAPTER 5

From Black and White to Multicultural Ecumenism 1996-2014

By my reckoning, my current address is the twentieth home I have lived in since arriving in England as a mid-teenager. Since being married in 1974, Novelette and I are now on our seventeenth. That's one every 2.3 years but it includes a lengthy spell of thirteen years at one. We have travelled and moved with great frequency, some of it at our own volition, some occasioned by my church assigning me to pastor and the challenges of finding accommodation in an ecclesial system that did not have manses. Here we were again in 1996 faced with one of those house moves.

Having moved regularly, it was not the most daunting of tasks. I have lived in Birmingham, the Black Country, Kent, Oxford, Rotherham and Sheffield up to that time and the prospect of a move back to Birmingham, at our, not my church's behest, was to be taken in our stride. Not so for our young children who had spent most of their formative years in Sheffield. For them, much more than Novelette and me, Sheffield was really home, with a Yorkshire accent to boot.

Well, the task of moving went reasonably smoothly.

We found a rented house in Birmingham while we tried to sell our Sheffield one and after a year we were able to move to a lovely mature bungalow near the well-known Spaghetti Junction. Schools were sourced for the children and finding a local church was easy since the Church of God of Prophecy at Aberdeen Street, Winson Green has been my home church since arriving in England in 1968. Novelette quickly found a job too as project manager at a mental health initiative.

With careful thinking and action and some perseverance, everything slotted neatly into place for us, including the assurance that I could continue to pursue my PhD research into understanding the black Churches better in terms of their historical moorings and their future as part of the British national church.

Something I had not reckoned on was the interpretation some would put on my resignation from the offices of pastor and bishop – some still call me pastor and I continue to hold the title of bishop, though not in post as pastor or bishop. I was to later learn that for some, my resignation was tantamount to a betrayal, dereliction of duty, backsliding, deserting the church! Quite apart from the members of my local church in Sheffield and district five, people who had no direct connection with me still were affected, some hurt. I had voluntarily laid down posts that were viewed by the masses as divine appointments from which one must not resign; as one person put it to me, 'a true pastor can't resign; how dat work?'. It is undoubtedly true that most pastors and bishops in the Church of God of Prophecy in England would not dream of resigning to go to something else; this would be due to at least two reasons.

First, many feel that these appointments were irreversible appointments based on divine callings and therefore to resign is to be in rebellion against God and the church. A second reason was that in the short history of the Church of God of Prophecy and other black-led churches in Britain, credible options were few, if a pastor or bishop wanted to maintain a certain lifestyle and financial security. By the grace of God I had options. Leaving my positions, however, started me on an odyssey that was to develop into a theological and psychological chasm that would prove challenging to maintain connections. However challenging this proved, I think there will be more and more pastors and bishops who will find themselves in a similar place to me back in the mid-1990s. It will be interesting to see what choices they make.

My reason for returning to Birmingham was as the new Executive Director of the Centre for Black and White Christian Partnership. I started the first week in September 1996 and for the first month my venerable predecessor was asked to be available to me as I settled in. I did not need him for a whole month and after week two he scarcely came into the office. This was a whole new world of ministry for me. The Centre's remit was multifaceted but revolved mainly around a Certificate in Theology programme that since its inception in the 1970s was offered to black leaders in the main but available to any who wished to study it; and was validated by Birmingham University.

Around this certificate course was a much wider and ambitious programme of cultural engagement of 'black and white' people and churches, or, as I came to call it, 'intercultural ecumenism'. Based in the lovely, picturesque grounds of the Selly Oak Colleges, the bungalow in which the Centre existed was a refuge for many who looked for a culturally, ethnically and denominationally mixed environment. It was also home to many forlorn students of nearby and sometimes not so nearby universities who felt their supervisors did not understand them or their subjects. Early on, I realised that this was going to be a challenging role continuing what its originators called at the outset in 1978, 'a project in partnership between black and white Christians'. My first challenge though was a financial one. Had I known the extent of the financial woes of the Centre I have wondered if I would have accepted the job. My conclusion is still yes.

I threw myself into being Director of the Centre for Black and White Christian Partnership – immersing myself into a new job was the only way I knew. My small staff team made up of employees and volunteers must have thought a whirlwind had hit them. Among them were Mavis Braham my PA, a bundle of energy and font of knowledge; and Senior Apostle John Adegoke my Finance Officer who also happened to be a minister in the Cherubim and Seraphim Church. Mavis, best remembered for her 'clean desk policy' that meant never leaving files on her desk at the end of each day, was to move on eventually and be succeeded by Gerry Bryan as my PA. Gerry was an organiser par excellence! I still use her 'bring forward' diary filing system to this day and my mobile number is still the one she negeotiated and set up back then. The relaxed, jovial yet cerebral ways of my predecessor Dr Patrick Kalilombe gave way to a level of activism that even for me as the Director felt daunting. Being Director of a Centre such as this meant being multi-intentional and innovative and I was from the outset looking for ways in which I could build on what had gone before.

I was Director of Studies for the Theology course with responsibility to find new students and liaise with the university; tutor, supervise students and staff, and increasingly consultant to a wide variety of people and organisations that wanted to engage with Black Christianity. I loved every moment of every day and had a Chair (Rt Rev'd Dr Rupert Hoare, Anglican suffragan Bishop of Dudley), and Board that was every bit as supportive as I could ever expect. They gave me room to lead.

The Centre for Black and White Christian Partnership was set in the beautiful Selly Oak/Bourneville area and was among well-established units like Westhill (Teacher Training) College and several others that formed the Selly Oak Colleges Federation. The Federation was gradually being drawn closer to the University of Birmingham, which eventually gobbled it all up for a notional £1 we were told. I guess much of the Federation became untenable and was, for all intents and purposes, taken over by the University.

En route to absorption by the University, I was for a while Vice-President of the Federation; which was nice even though highly symbolic since there were few duties not undertaken by the President of the Federation. These were heady days working among many impressive academicians and when added to this was driving each morning to such a beautiful setting where the occasional fox was to be seen moving across beautifully manicured lawns and well coiffured plants, bushes and trees; well it was a great joy to go to work.

One of my first observation was the way the Centre attempted to live up to its name of a Black and White Christian Partnership. This was done principally by having one black and one white as co-chairs of the board; then the board of twelve was also divided equally black and white. It did not take me long to recognise that numerical equality between black and white did not mean equal power and influence on the Centre's governing board. While the white board members were invariably retired or semi-retired professionals, with few exceptions it was as though the black board members had been chosen on the basis of whoever the Centre could find.

It was clear to me that insufficient care was taken over the choices of the black board members and it became one of my early tasks to work with the chairmen to rotate some members off the board and replace them with suitably qualified black individuals. Within a relatively short time into my directorship, we had successfully recruited an effective black and white board. This became totemic of relationships in other spheres of the Centre's life; equal numbers did not necessarily equate with equal power unless the people making up the numbers were suitably qualified and able to perform the tasks for which they were there. Making the board stronger, paid rich dividends as the revamped board provided excellent scrutiny and support for the agenda I pursued.

One of my most interesting interactions started when I received a call from (the late) Professor Michael Goulder, inviting me to lunch. I did not know who he was initially but soon discovered that he was a very influential figure in the Centre's flagship Certificate in Theology course (CIT). He was a biblical scholar based at the University of Birmingham and had taught on the CIT for some considerable time.

Professor Goulder had been a Church of England clergy who lost his faith but continued lecturing on the bible. I was informed that when he publically renounced his Christian faith and ministry in the Church of England, he was a lecturer on the CIT and offered his resignation. However, his CIT students, among them black church pastors and bishops, persuaded him not to leave. They somehow rationalised that his task of helping them better understand the Bible was one he could do whether or not he believed in the God of the Bible; quite an interesting rationale for a constituency usually thought of as fundamentalists.

The students said they would continue to pray for him, but he should continue teaching. And he did! By the time I arrived as Director he was no longer teaching but was sufficiently interested in the project to call me and made an appointment to meet me. He seemed to have no agenda except to give me the benefit of his observations concerning the Centre and to wish me well. I still think that was a magnanimous gesture for a man who declared himself an agnostic.

The Centre's pioneering CIT course was studied part time one week-end per month over two years and covered Old and New Testament, Mission and study skills which was needed by many but not all of the mature students that attended. Old and New Testament studies followed classic biblical studies format one would expect to encounter in the first third of a bachelor's degree in Biblical Studies, which was the academic worth of the CIT. But the CIT allowed for a great deal of enculturation in that students, overwhelmingly but not exclusively Black African and Caribbean of varying ages and of both genders, were encouraged to use material and examples from their church context in doing their work. While that may have been challenging in Old and New Testament essays, Mission studies lent itself wonderfully to enculturation, and when various African and Caribbean meals were thrown into the mix, fellowshipping and studying at the Centre was a glorious experience.

The Mission module included visits to different churches most Sunday mornings, Saturdays for Sabbatarian visits, of the monthly study weekends; and my main contribution was to develop this into becoming a standalone module with credits within the CIT. Students would write up their experiences of these visits to churches of different denominations and reflect theologically and missiologically on what they learned in light of their experiences of their own traditions.

Attached to the CIT without being formally part of its assessment framework was a regular Theology Forum with oppositional speakers as a feature. All in all this was an innovative certificate in theology programme which I enjoyed leading and developing. For a while, I held out hope of adding a Diploma as level 2 and a level 3 to complete the Bachelor's degree, but never managed to get those approved by the University before the Centre closed in 2002. Several other programmes were developed in counselling and legal studies.

The Centre was a hive of activity partly because it boasted a library that was the envy of many study centres because of our collection of specialist books in the field of black religious studies. We were busy also because it was one of its type for many miles where one could find an unapologetically stimulating academic and intellectual 'black space' to study and relax and consult. The Centre was a black space not because there were no non-blacks there, but because it was a decidedly black-affirming space. I had concluded that if black and white were to seriously be in partnership, then the black partner who was currently the weaker of the two needed strengthening. And I decided not to be meanie-mouthed about recognising that need.

And so within a relatively short space of time black affirmation and empowerment became my unofficial motto as a director. In addition to doing the routine duties of a director; meeting people, answering queries, dealing with the press, running courses and programmes, speaking and lecturing and such like I launched on a programme of black affirmation and empowerment that was to define my time as the Centre's Director.

As mentioned above, I started with the membership of the Board and with the backing of an excellent Chair and his black Vice-Chair, we maintained a high level of Board leadership working with me as director. I was determined to make a difference to black and white Christian relationship by strengthening black people in as many ways as was in my power.

An early area I wanted to address was trying to answer the question, why were there so few black British theological writers that could be read and quoted in lecture notes and student essays? Most of what existed were writings about not by us, and as the fabled African proverb goes, 'Until the lions write the story of the hunt, it will always glorify the hunter'. In sum, people should tell their own stories. After many discussions it was decided that we would attempt to publish an anthology of sermons by black preachers.

As I began to float the idea I came across some interesting reactions. Most common was something like, 'black preachers do not write sermons because they come from an oral culture'.

Well, maybe, but I was determined to find enough black pastors to make up an anthology and find a mainstream publisher to boot! I mentioned this project in practically every conversation, talk, presentation, lecture, sermon I did for several months until out of the blue one day a woman heard me and asked to discuss it with me. She turned out to be a commissioner with a publisher and found the idea of an anthology of black British preachers a novel one – excuse the pun, but it was.

Cassell Publishing Company agreed to publish the anthology subject to their usual caveats in relation to quality, sales potential, timing and such like. We decided to have twenty contributors and to achieve that I found I had to approach double that; but get them I did and the book was titled 'Preaching with Power - Sermons by black Preachers'. The inclusion of 'power' in the title was to illustrate an attribute I think is self-evident in black preaching which is almost always more forceful than subtle.

I even chose a cover picture of a black preacher with clenched fist, perspiration running down his forehead, in a caption of the dynamism of black preaching. During the editing phase of Preaching with Power, I was contacted by the publishers enquiring if I minded them putting forward one of the sermons as an entrant in the annual Preacher of the Year competition that was operated by the College of Preachers and the Times Newspaper. Did I mind? Of course, I didn't mind!

The request was music to my ears although I had never heard of this competition. I saw this as the first fruit of this literary initiative and an opportunity to bring black preaching to mainstream attention. I may have begun by wanting black literary resources in the Centre, but the wider vision was to have a book like this in libraries and on study courses everywhere. The publishers did not ask me which of the twenty sermons I would like entered, they were clear that the one they wanted to enter was by Pastor Ian Sweeney, a Seventh Day Adventist Minister from Sheffield titled, 'Skin deep Christianity'. This was the sermon he had preached in the Together in Unity ecumenical black-led celebration I had chaired in 1997 and had asked Pastor Sweeney if he would kindly write it up for this anthology.

Skin deep Christianity was entered into the Preacher of the Year competition - and after a lengthy process, it won! So there were these two big wins for me and the Centre's work: we published the anthology in 1998 and one of the sermons won the National Preacher of the Year competition on the first occasion (so I was told) a black preacher had participated in it. We had begun to lay to rest the stereotype that black preachers were oral, did not, could not write sermons and only knew how to preach extemporaneously.

I warmed to the reception 'Preaching with Power' got, and decided to utilise the word 'power' for another two anthologies; Sisters with Power and Praying with Power. Sisters with Power contains articles by (mostly black) women on various topics and is still a great read for anyone wanting to gain insights into the minds of intelligent black women of the church at the start of the second millennium. Praying with Power contains reflections by black Christians on the discipline of prayer.

By the time these were published, Cassell Publishing Limited had morphed into Continuum; and they agreed to publish these edited works under my name. These latter two anthologies were published simultaneously in 2000. This was seriously hard work and I pledged that three edited anthologies was enough for anyone. Never again, I said. I remember failing to meet two scripts submission deadlines and was still up at 3AM one Friday night so that I could mail the manuscripts as hard copies and on floppy discs in the Saturday morning post. As hard work as these were, we now had three books by British black Christians in the public domain and it was a joy to see them taking their places in the religious departments of libraries up and down the country.

These three books were revolutionary in two significant ways. First, almost at a stroke, we had managed to get forty black Christians published in the mainstream, with almost everyone previously unpublished. The experience I gained as a new editor was invaluable but the experience each of them gained of writing for publication and seeing their names alongside their articles was exhilarating – I know because many of them told me so. This has led to several of them building on that experience and going on to write and publish independently of me. That's what I meant by empowerment! Second, I had deliberately adopted a philosophy of looking for writers from across the church, as was befitting of the Centre's multidenominational work. I ensured I approached potential writers from historic and new black churches, Oneness and Trinitarian Pentecostals, Seventh Day Adventists and more, in a deliberate act of multi-denominational collaboration, if not subtle subversion.

The Chairmen and Trustees of the Centre for Black and White Christian Partnership were wonderfully supportive and at the launch of these books could be seen purring with pride. This was Black empowerment in support of Black and White Christian partnership based on my emerging philosophy that if we are were to succeed in establishing true partnership it would be based on mutuality and equality, not on benevolence and pity extended from articulate whites to well-meaning but incapable Black partners. The talent I discovered in the contributors for these three anthologies were not created by me; just discovered, engaged and guided, where this was needed.

Having developed an early appetite for boosting the literary stock of the black religious community and the Centre, and continuing to work with academic and religious leaders another project emerged. Not long after I arrived at the Centre, I discovered that there was a Black Theology Group that met once per month. I started attending and got to know the main leaders, among them; Dr George Mulrain, Dr Emmanuel Lartey, Rev'd Inderjit Bhogal and Rev'd Dr Kate Coleman, herself a PhD candidate at the time.

Soon, it seemed sensible and appropriate to everyone that the forum should be convened at the Centre and indeed, the forum became a part of the Centre's work programme with my staff taking responsibility for sending out reminders and helping to coordinate speakers and, over time, I assumed the chair. The Forum Planning Group discussed the possibility of publishing a Journal of Black Theology as a literary expression of the Forum, providing publication possibilities to the excellent academic papers that were being presented monthly at the Forum. Ideas like this one tend to assume a life of their own and before we knew it, I, with the same zeal I perused the first anthology, began to explore the feasibility of publishing a journal including costs, timescale, and publisher. We discovered there was no black theology journal in existence anywhere in the world and so became even more determined to make this a reality.

After much excitement and hard work, we launched the journal late 1998. Being at the time a PhD candidate at Sheffield University I knew that their publication associate, Sheffield Academic Press, published journals; they kindly agreed to be the publisher of our new journal. We settled on the title: Black Theology in Britain – A Journal of Contextual Praxis. I became Chair of the Editorial Board, Dr Emmanuel Lartey became its Editor. We made a formidable team with an excellent Editorial Committee, an Editorial Advisory Board and we were supported by key institutional backers, like the Church of England's Committee for Minority Ethnic Anglican Concerns.

Launching the first Black Theology Journal was such a proud moment for us all and with the full backing of my Chairs and Trustees at the Centre, I spearheaded formal launches in Birmingham and London. Mainly as a consequence of the Centre's closure in 2002, but also because of a failure to secure sufficient levels of subscriptions and support from our natural constituency, the black Churches, in time the journal moved in different editorial and marketing directions. Our original intentions to mainly grow black British theologians through exposure to the rigours of an academic journal turned out not to be entirely compatible with the high level of academic acumen required for such a journal. The launch of a journal of Black Theology in Britain was no mean feat.

My resignation as Chair of the Editorial Board in 2002 and prior to that the departure of the original editor signalled a shift that took the journal on to more sound economic and academic footing, further away from our original idealist ideology. It was renamed, 'Black Theology – An International Journal' under a new editor, chair, board and publisher, and at the time of writing, fifteen years on, I have no formal links with the journal;

but mighty proud of the part I played with others in launching the original journal; and of course it continues to feature black British contributors, just not restricted to them.

Within two years of being at the Centre for Black and White Christian Partnership I had got the bits firmly between my teeth on the literary publishing front. In addition to the power series of books that first appeared in 1998 and the Journal of Black Theology, I edited a popular monthly newsletter, 'Partnership News', an equally popular 'Ten tips for partnership' leaflet; and began to think hard about responding to increasing calls for a tool that made it easier to identify black Churches in Birmingham and beyond. This need became more apparent as I and others pressed various parties for greater black inclusion and participation. The inevitable response was, 'I do not know where to find them'. This was, in my view, more often than not, an excuse to maintain the status quo by exclusion supported by minimum effort or sometimes none at all.

It was, however, true that black churches had grown in such a dynamic and dispersed manner since the 1950s that whilst there was a small number of national denominations, the majority were independent churches, the details of which were difficult to find even for those of us working in the field of networking them. When we discussed this situation at the Centre the idea emerged that we might compile and publish a Black Church Directory. We already possessed a significant contact list of independent churches and were aware that national headquarters held information about their local churches. There were also records of an assortment of Black ecumenical and umbrella groups such as the African and Caribbean Evangelical Alliance, all of which proved to be a good starting point for information gathering.

Our initial attempt was earnest but not very professional and I had to admit that we did not have the expertise in-house to compile a directory. A white volunteer began the process but I soon discovered some of the pitfalls of a well-intentioned white man compiling a black church directory! The first advert for submissions that appeared in the Centre's newsletter indulged in a bit of harmless banter, or so he thought, about some of the exotic names used by black churches. Well, the complaints came pouring in from readers: 'How dare you poke fun at our churches?' seemed to be the rhetorical question. I took that on the chin and made sure it never happened again.

I decided to up the game concerning the Black Church Directory by seeking to source funding to engage a professional compiler and publisher. It was my good fortune that at the Church of England's Church Urban Fund as director was Angela Sarkis, a black woman with historic roots in the Pentecostal tradition. Angela was most accommodating to my approach to consider funding the first national Black Church Directory, and the African and Caribbean Evangelical Alliance's Director, Katie Kirby, was equally willing to share their contacts database and be a partner in this initiative. It took some assembling, but we developed a great partnership between our three organisations, found a company led by Folake Segun, of African British descent, and published the first 'Directory of Black Majority Churches' just before the Centre closed in 2002.

It was a great achievement that attracted a lot of attention and although we all knew this was by no means a comprehensive listing of black churches in Britain, it was a worthy attempt that, at a minimum, removed the 'I do not know where to find them' excuse or reason for non-inclusion of black Christians or churches in mainstream activities. Two hard copy versions of the directory was published, the second in 2005, and I eventually decided that an online version was preferable. Today the online 'Black and Multicultural Directory' sits proudly online as a free resource for anyone wishing to access it, now supported by Churches Together in England, for which I work. But it all started at the Centre for Black and White Christian Partnership during a period of publishing mania!

My six years as Director of the Centre were filled with excitement: it launched me on a new career path, meeting new people, sharing in and helping to shape individual and group studies and outcomes and offering spiritual guidance. Excitement also extended, at times, to potentially more mundane aspects like travelling and meetings that allowed me space the think, especially when staffing and resources issues challenged the peace.

One of the highlights of each year was the annual graduation when Certificate in Theology (CIT) students who had been awarded their certificates by the University of Birmingham joined other Centre students on courses, mainly counselling, to receive their awards. Because the CIT was an undergraduate course, the University did not make awards, so the Centre filled that gap. Those who wished to continue studying to diploma and degree levels would transfer to the University if they passed the CIT with a sufficiently high mark to progress to what was effectively year two of the three year degree, or six years part-time. Several students did so successfully, the occasional few going on to complete masters and in even fewer cases, doctorates.

The Centre's annual graduation was extra special because many of the successful students had never before achieved academic awards. The expressions on some faces had to be seen to be believed and understood. Pride and happiness writ large. Their achievement in meeting the requirements of the various exam boards could not be underestimated and showed again and again that the real differences between people were opportunities. Many African and Caribbean people, because of the challenges of migration and settlement, did not get the full range of opportunities open to later generations. Notwithstanding the level of certification, for these graduates their award was as special as achieving a PhD. I was so happy and felt so proud to help make so many dreams come true.

The Centre under my leadership excelled in the area of black empowerment, as an intentional act. I became more and more convinced that to be good partners in this Black and White Christian Partnership, black Christians needed to be strong in all necessary and possible ways. Partnership, I was sure would not thrive on black weakness, or white pity and benevolence towards black people; and I embraced the principle that power is never given, it is only ever taken. I was after a partnership of equals.

An obvious area for strengthening was bringing black and white Christians together in ecumenical, theological or missional reflection. I found black leaders in Birmingham and elsewhere to be somewhat apprehensive, even timid and lacking in confidence when it came to engaging with their white ministerial counterparts. I saw this clearly on several occasions at the theological forums the Centre convened, which usually featured white theological experts with there being few black ones at the time. There, during theological discussions some black participants would tend toward being quiet while some would have been well advised to adhere to the maxim, 'Better to remain silent and be thought a fool, than to speak and remove all doubt'.

I believed that this disparity between black and white had little or nothing to do with innate ability or spirituality and everything to do with opportunities. White ministers, on a whole, because they belonged to the 'historic' churches where training was a requisite, they got that training. Black churches on the other hand did not insist on academic theological training. They depended more on 'calling' or gifting. Invariably, if it were a matter of style, black won hands down; but on matters of substance, because of inadequate training for black ministers, white won. For me this was eminently fixable. We needed to emphasise ministerial and theological training among black churches, which as a process had already begun both in Centres like my own and in some of the churches themselves.

There is a Caribbean, probably Jamaican, maxim that 'You have to learn to dance ayard before you dance abroad'. Applying this meant that black ministers needed to become comfortable in their own selves before they would be comfortable in the company of others. Not only were some black Pentecostal leaders not comfortable in the company of white mainstream trained clergy, they were not comfortable in the presence of theologically trained black ones either and as a consequence, we struggled to get those pastors to attend the Black Theology Forum. I initiated a strategy to help by convening some facilitated black and white conversations at the Centre while simultaneously orchestrating the strengthening of the Council of Black-led Churches that had been in existence for some time but had waned in recent times.

With assistance, I managed to assemble some of the most denominationally diverse gatherings; Asian, black and white,

Trinitarian and Oneness, historic mainline and Seventh Day Adventist, House Church, Pentecostals and Charismatics. These were unlikely gatherings. In one meeting, a black minister of one denomination that had been highly separatist explained his reason for attending as, 'Winston Churchill said, jaw jaw is better than war war'. Quietly behind the scenes I would seek to embolden some of the black church leaders, encouraging them to speak up in discussions. But the need for further 'black space' where black could speak unapologetically to black was clear; and since the Black Theology Forum did not attract the majority of black Pastors, I focussed on the Council of Black-led Churches as a possible rallying point.

If the Council of Black-led Churches were to be a tool of black ministers empowerment, it needed to come under the control of those of us who could use it in that way. Some leaders, who had not been part of the Council, and I sought to influence it; and eventually the leadership that had been largely politically rather that ministerially led, fell into the hands of bone fide church leaders. I felt that if a core of black church leaders could become emboldened by having their confidence strengthened through robust conversations in the Council of Black-led Churches, we could, from there, export confidence to such as the black and multi-denominational meetings we were holding; and if not immediately, then later. It is difficult to say for sure whether this affected those conversations at the Centre for Black and White Christian Partnership, but I began to see signs that individuals were growing in confidence. I had resisted the encouragement to become Chairman of the Council, opting instead to offer myself as vice-chair and served in that voluntary position assisting and empowering the Chairman, the dynamic young Bishop Derek Webley of the New Testament Church of God who was to go on to lead in a cutting edge manner.

Eventually I served as Chairman for five years when Derek stepped down and during those ten years or so between 1997-2007, the Council played a leading role in the fight against gangs, drugs, guns and knives. I will return to my time as chair of CBLC later. We sought to support young people in various ways such as giving awards at our annual banquet, worked with the local council and police, some of us worked alongside the health service. I became board member of a few organisations, acceding to Chairman of a large Primary Care Trust, turning over some £500,000,000 per annum! Council colleagues fared equally impressively in other spheres. By bringing people into an affirming black space from where we engaged with the world, the fruit of our strategy was clear to behold, including religious partnerships in Birmingham's Church Leaders Group and Birmingham Faith Leaders Group, and others. These were fruitful years.

In the midst of great success at the Centre, I attended the World Council of Churches General Assembly in Harare, Zimbabwe in 1998. The main purpose of my attending was to convene a workshop on the model of the Centre for Black and White Christian Partnership. Among those who signed up for the workshop were some South Africans. As I began to develop my theory of empowering black people, sometimes separately from whites, there was a walk-out by the South Africans. Later I learned that they felt I was advocating segregation, an ideology that had brought them so much grief in their country. I understood fully their position, however, believed still that in order to have healthy black and white partnerships we must have mutual respect and that comes when both parties felt self-respected which is then brought to bear in the poise and posture and contribution they bring to the partnership. Sometimes, I believe, strengthening needs to be done separately.

My visit to Zimbabwe has stayed in my mind for other reasons too. Among them, just how reminiscent Zimbabwe and her people were of my native Jamaica. Added to that, both Nelson Mandela, recently released from prison, and Robert Mugabe addressed the WCC General Assembly; Mandela to express thanks for the support the WCC had given to the ANC struggle against Apartheid; and Mugabe spoke as President of the country. I do not recall much of the contents of either man's speech, but I came away with a feeling that President Mugabe out-spoke President Mandela massively. I became a Mugabe fan instantly and I declared myself a honorary Zimbabwean ever since!

I remember the General Assembly for another reason. Something that happened in one discussion where a speaker representing an African indigenous church seeking membership of the WCC but denied on the grounds of their continuing to practice polygamy. The representative said something to the effect that he could not fathom how it was that the European churches that effectively dictated WCC policy could deny his church membership because they practised polygyny that was 'nowhere in the bible forbidden' while they themselves allowed membership to churches that approved of the practice of homosexuality that was 'everywhere in the bible forbidden'. Whatever the rights or wrongs of the points of view, I was pleased to see and hear an African boldly standing up for himself and his church in such a setting as the World Council of Churches General Assembly.

An international initiative that thrived at the Centre for Black and White Christian Partnership was a fund-raising drive I launched to help my Alma Mata, Paul Mountain All-Age School, in Jamaica, my school before coming to England in 1968. I found some willing allies among the Centre's volunteers; none more so than Carol Penn, a Quaker who both contributed personally and helped organise the campaign. Together with people from outside the Centre, including fellow Paul Mountarians, we raised sufficient to build a small computer lab and furnished it with ten new computers and a printer. I was the proudest of men when I was able to visit the school and open the lab to great acclaim and national press coverage.

By the time of the opening of the computer lab, I had achieved my PhD and so was a kind of homeboy made good. For me this was a genuine and heartfelt thank you to the people and their children and place that had given me life and to show gratitude to God for opening doors for me to leave and get an education and be in a position to raise funds to help the new generations of youths. I hoped that by helping to provide a computer lab I was contributing to their development and advancement to better lives. Sadly, I was unable to find an internet supplier so the children from this remote country place could surf the world wide net. I hoped that in years to come that would happen. I so enjoyed my trips to my old school and took opportunity to play cricket on the pitch I played as a child. I raised thousands of pounds that contributed to its development in several ways to improve the quality of life and the learning experience of the children in my old district.

The issue of funding was a problem at the Centre for one reason or another. As I've mentioned previously, it had struggled with funding for years and had launched appeals repeatedly. The last significant funding appeal happened shortly before I took up the job as director and there was a sense that sources had become tired, while some previously generous donors had made it clear that they had given their last. Probably the most challenging aspect of the funding situation of the Centre for me was seeing the end of year accounts and being confronted with the stark reality that the bulk of the Centre's income came from white donors. So, here I was, a proud black man, leading a Centre that served a majority black clientele, and increasingly developing projects that were black benefiting in the interest of empowering the blacks for better Black and White Christian Partnership; and yet we looked to white people to provide the money to make all this happen. This did not sit comfortably with me.

Of course, if my prognosis were correct and the blacks in the partnership were the weaker partner then it stood to reason that they were also poorer than whites. But black churches in Britain, even in the 1990s, had a reputation for growing faster than white ones, so why shouldn't they put some of the income generated from their swelling numbers towards supporting a Centre that was dedicating so much towards their development and empowerment. Try as I might in my six years at the Centre, I never managed to shift the funding profile significantly although we began to create some funding from student fees and from the Higher Education Funding Council for England (HEFCE).

Whilst I candidly accepted my failure to get funding from black churches to support the Centre, succeeding in getting some of the money that came from HEFCE was a great achievement because the University and the Further Education College we dealt with were very happy receiving and retaining the fees attached to the Centre's students and because HEFCE did not deal with the Centre directly for a long time that funding stream was concealed from me and I presumed my predecessors. Once I made it clear that I knew they got funding and I wanted the Centre's share, they played ball! Me born a country, but me no fool.

Before moving on from my time at the Centre for Black and White Christian Partnership, I want to share a funny story. We had many lighter moments at the Centre over the years I was Director – like the time when a member of staff (identity obscured for obvious reasons) diligently labelled every item in the storeroom and labelled one 'paper bowels', instead of 'paper bowls'. We all fell about laughing.

Then prior to one of the Certificate in Theology course weekends, I was contacted jointly by the Bible Society in Britain and the Bible Society of the West Indies, based in Jamaica, concerning their plans to pilot an audio recording of the Bible in Jamaican (Patois). I had grown up speaking Patois but it was always viewed as a dialect for private use amongst Jamaicans, and then only in unofficial settings. The Queen's English was the official Jamaican language spoken by all respectable citizens, especially the educated ones. I was keen to learn more about this attempt to produce an audio of the Bible in Patois. I had even agreed to help launch the pilot in Birmingham and had arranged a seminar event at a local church, the Cannon Street Memorial Baptist Church in Handsworth. In fact, it was in that church that I made an observation that was to have future consequences when I told the white pastor of what was a black-majority church I so loved the building that I felt I could pastor there! More later.

On the Friday before the Saturday seminar, I received a copy of the audio recording; a portion of John's Gospel. In front of the class of students, I played the tape and immediately collapsed on the floor in a fit of uncontrollable laughter upon hearing John's Gospel in my native Jamaican. It felt like this was a wrong response but I couldn't help myself. Later I was told that this was not an unusual response upon hearing the Bible in one's mother tongue that hitherto was considered unsuitable, too common, for the Word of God. It is also the case that English was once considered too common for the Word of God to be translated from Latin into. People lost their lives for doing so. At least that fate was not on show here.

Ecumenism Part 2 – CTBI/CTE

In 2001/2 negotiations were intense as the Centre for Black and White Christian Partnership's Board, led by Chairman Rt Rev'd Dr Rupert Hoare and the irrepressible Rev'd Dr Michael Taylor, acting in his role as President of Selly Oak Colleges - of which the Centre was a part - sought to close the Centre in the best possible way, including relocating its work in other institutions. There were going to be inevitable redundancies of my staff and my own status was uncertain. Michael told me in no uncertain terms that he was not at all concerned about me, because I would be snapped up by some organisation or other. His main concern was for the welfare of my staff members - they were my concern too.

We managed a smooth shutdown with admin staff redundancies; the Centre's theological training work transferred with myself and one other part-time academic staff to the University of Birmingham, the Counselling courses with two part-time staff transferred to Bourneville College of Further Education, and the ecumenical work was transferred to Churches Together in Britain and Ireland (CTBI). The arrangement concerning me were a little tricky because the university expressed a wish for me to continue with them as Director of a new Centre for Black Theology. I agreed to set it up, but did not wish to pursue an academic career within the university.

I wanted to continue with the intercultural ecumenism I had got to love and that meant working out a deal with Churches Together in Britain and Ireland. After setting up the Centre for Black Theology in the university, I applied for the post of Ecumenical Advisor at CTBI and got it after an interview. With the new job came the task of integrating a fledgling Black Support

Group that had been recently set up within CTBI for black churches with the portfolio handed over from the Centre. The downside of this was that CTBI did not have the funds to employ me full-time. So from the autumn of 2002 I was employed half-time as Secretary for Minority Ethnic Christian Affairs (MECA). This led to a prolonged period of creatively looking for work to make up my half-time earning.

Some time before the closure of the Centre there was a national leadership selection process in my church, the Church of God of Prophecy, for the role of National 'Overseer' (sic). At the time I was well ensconced in my role as Director of the Centre and had no desire for denominational leadership. However, and much to my surprise, my name was submitted into the selection process. Whoever did it did not consult me – there was no requirement to do so. I thought long and hard before agreeing to the request from the National Office to submit my CV, but after conversations with my wife Novelette and a few close friends I decided to do so. I reasoned that although I stood no realistic chance of being appointed, given the problematic nature of our relationship, I could at least lay down a marker concerning what I perceived the challenges to be and what I thought could be done to create a progressive and upwardly mobile church: spiritually, socially, culturally, politically and economically relevant for its time.

In agreeing to be a candidate for the national leader role I made one condition: that I wanted the opportunity to address the gathered selection panel, which was essentially all the licensed and ordained ministers of the Church of God of Prophecy in England. I was informed by the leaders of the process that my request was reasonable but they would have to put it to the other two candidates. It was not clear from the administrators whether they objected to my request to speak, but they did not wish to avail themselves of that privilege. It was decided therefore that as they would not be addressing the gathered ministers on the day of selection, I could not be allowed to do so. With that, I said I would withdraw from the process since if in addition to our calling, qualifications and experience the selection did not take into account the candidates' assessment of the current situation of the Church and our vision for its future I did not know on what basis the selection would be made. 'Maybe the colours of our eyes?' I mused. There was quite some effort made to persuade me to stay in the process, but I was resolute in my decision. I did not much like the selection process and it went ahead without me.

Six months out from the close of the Centre for Black and White Christian Partnership, I wrote to the national overseer of the Church of God of Prophecy, stating that although I did not know how things would work out when the Centre closed, I would be interested in discussing a possible return to pastoral work. But I suspect that six years after resigning as pastor and district overseer with all the discomfiture that caused many in my church, the matter of the selection process for National 'Overseer', my close identification with the wider church world; some may have considered me as having lost my denominational 'tribal mark' and therefore unfit to be the custodian or defender of the church's core teachings and polity. I was never told I was unsuitable to be pastor again but I was never invited to discuss where I might make a return to pastoral or supervisory work.

My sense of estrangement from my church continued to build based on some real life experiences. When some years later I actually applied for a vacant pastor's position, I was invited to an interview and a few weeks later informed by letter that the job had been given to another candidate. This person had no comparable pastor or overseer experience but apparently did not have 'conditions' attached as I had so would be able to devote their time unconditionally to the church. It did not escape my notice that the new pastor took up post and continued to work secularly part-time. My 'condition' was to make clear that were I to be offered the job, I would not give up my part-time position at Churches Together. I subsequently offered twice to help out voluntarily in churches that were in interregnum only to be politely turned down both times – my services were surplus to requirement.

The risk of alienation from my roots has been a real and present one from the day in 1996 that I voluntarily moved in a different direction from denominational domestication to working in the wider church and kingdom of God. At my induction into the role of Director of the Centre for Black and White Christian Partnership, my pastoral mentor Bishop T A McCalla said, 'Joseph, don't let them spoil you'. Maybe they had. But I was enjoying being spoilt. It had been personally, spiritually, philosophically and intellectually stimulating and I would not have swapped it for the world.

Truth is that I had moved on in my theological thinking and would not be a good defender of the traditional or classical, Pentecostal articles of faith embraced by my church such as 'initial evidence' (the teaching that a person must 'speak unknown tongues' as proof that baptism in the Spirit has occurred); so my church was probably right to view me with some suspicion. I still regarded myself as 'Pentecostal' but a different kind of Pentecostal; neither a cessationist or an essentialist, but believing that all the gifts of the Spirit are available to the entire church yet none of the gifts are a must for every Christian. Had I become pastor, or indeed National 'Overseer', I would have sought to effect progressive, transformational changes to church doctrines and practices as they stood – changes I still believed were necessary if my church was to make progress.

I held the belief that the Church of God of Prophecy in the United Kingdom needed root and branch de- and re-construction culturally, doctrinally and theologically and that to accomplish this the UK Church needed to declare UDI from its parent body in the US. So I guess the organisation's gatekeepers had reasons to fear my leading one of its congregations or to actively operate as a bishop again. I have accepted and am at complete peace with the fact that my church and me are in different places. But still no need for a divorce.

My move from the Centre for Black and White Christian Partnership to Churches Together in Britain and Ireland (CTBI), via the University of Birmingham was almost seamless. But then I have never had much problem moving on. A significant bonus was that from the outset CTBI, based in London, agreed to home working for me so I did not have the additional challenge of a house move – something my family may well have not welcomed. On the other hand, had a move to London been on the cards it would have represented a homecoming for my wife Novelette who grew up in Harlesden.

Still, the job was half time and on a moderate salary; so moving to the expensive south was not seriously considered. But there was a significant difference between my role at the Centre and my new job as Secretary of MECA at Churches Together. This was highlighted in the interview process. I accidentally met one of the interviewees competing with me for the post and to put it mildly, she was surprised that I was interested in it. She took the view that she stood no chance against me, but wondered aloud why I would be interested in a job that was not a director level post. She had a point. After being head of an organisation, albeit a small one, why was I now willing to work as a mere member of staff?

I was to find that the move from 'Director' to 'Secretary' was significant in terms of responsibility and authority. And yet the value and quality of the work I did at the Centre was enhanced within Churches Together because it was now located within a larger national organisation. It was a trade off that was well worth the demotion. I may have come down a peg but the work went up a peg. The truth is I did not find the change problematic because I had become wedded to the work of intercultural ecumenism and supporting black Christianity to become strong and assert itself much more than I was wedded to being the boss.

I was helped enormously to make the transition to being a member of staff at Churches Together by having surely one of the best 'boss' one could wish for. The late Dr David Goodbourn, who went on to become President of the ecumenical training college, Luther King House in Manchester, was gentleness and wisdom personified. I have already mentioned how it is that in a country sometimes described as 'institutionally racist' I have had the counter-intuitive experience of white individuals proving pivotal to my progress at critical points in my life. Here was another example. Proving that white agency and black progress is not an oxymoron. David was just there, leading more by asking questions than by giving instructions. A white British Baptist, he readily accepted that in the area of black Pentecostal Churches in Britain he was not the expert, I was; and proceeded to provide a context within which I could develop my work knowing I had his full support, making whatever resources I needed available.

One of the interesting dilemma we faced was how I should be titled. This was the period immediately following my successful PhD viva voce and I was now not only 'Bishop' but 'Doctor' too. Was I to be presented to the world as plain Joe Aldred, Bishop Joe Aldred, Dr Joe Aldred, Dr Bishop Joe Aldred, or Bishop Dr Joe Aldred? It was David who pointed out that in these matters God should always come first; so 'bishop' came first and we decided that I would be styled, 'Bishop Dr Joe Aldred'. Initially it felt rather clumsy. I do not know for sure if we were first to use it, but this has now become a common designation.

Part time the new post may have been but I threw myself into it – as I have said before, this is the only way I know to work. I said often that I worked full time, Churches Together in Britain and Ireland paid me for half time. This was only partly true because from the outset I needed to find work to compensate for the fact that after six years on a full time salary at the Centre I was now taking home a halftime salary. I will return to my part time endeavours during the eleven years I worked halftime for Churches Together in Britain and Ireland and churches together in England, between 2002-2013.

Beginning my new role at Churches Together in 2002 I discovered a dynamic not unlike that which met me at the start of my tenure as director of the Centre; that is a group of black people working to achieve equality but some being demonstrably unsuitable for the task. I inherited a small core group with a Chairman. There were quarterly meetings and the attendees represented the black churches that were in membership of Churches Together in Wales, Ireland, Scotland and England, WISE, as they was sometimes referred to.

The remit of the group's work was to encourage equal participation of black churches in the ecumenical process through greater self and wider understandings between black and white led churches. But there was the inherent challenge of the quality of the people who attended meetings, and their abilities to enable these objectives. I need to say some of these black church representatives were excellent, the same, however, could not be said of all.

The group needed a new Chairperson than the one I inherited who had done a good job but was now clearly not best suited for the new phase of work with me as Secretary. Maybe I should explain that 'Secretary' did not mean taking notes; rather it took its name from the naming of the head of Churches Together who was called the General Secretary. Each departmental head therefore was called Secretary.

In addition to needing a new chair with whom I could work, we needed a name for the work that carried more weight, more positivity, than 'Black Christian Concerns' that sounded like a moaning charter. And it was clear to me that the churches that were existing members of Churches Together were mainly the smaller black churches that desired respect. The larger more self-confident black churches were not members.

The overwhelming majority of black churches were Pentecostal and Evangelical and viewed the Churches Together enterprise as liberal theologically and doctrinally. They found the Evangelical Alliance a more natural bedfellow. But, importantly, it was Churches Together and through it Free Churches Group membership that facilitated chaplaincy and church school acceptance for their children. For the larger black churches the liberalism outweighed the other factors and so the smaller churches occupied that black church space in the Churches Together.

It was a case of the tail wagging the dog in that at national set piece occasions when the black church was represented it was a minister from a small black church who did so because it was they who were Churches Together members. I soon devised a strategy to sort my three initial dilemmas: find a new chair, find a new name and remit for the work, and get the larger black churches into membership of Churches Together.

Finding a new chair for the new work was potentially challenging. The old chair was a lovely fellow and much loved and I did not have anything against him, just a feeling that I needed a fresh start with a new chair. I was mindful too of the Jamaican saying, 'New broom sweep clean, old broom know the corners'. Interestingly, the old chair did not belong to a member church of Churches Together and in that way pre-empted the direction of travel under my leadership and the remit that emerged to look and work beyond the existing membership. The intention was clear even if the means were not.

I convened a day of reflection on the way forward. We had excellent speakers, food and good company; but running through the day was a steely determination on my part to end up with a clear direction and a new chair. It was at this first public meeting that I met the person I call 'prophetess'; Rev'd Celia Apeagyei-Collins who headed the Rehoboth Foundation. Celia was a young woman of great spiritual insight based on biblical principles and she was to become an international speaker and a regular feature at events I organised.

We emerged from that day-long meeting with a vision, a new name and a new chair. To my joy we managed to steer clear of making racism the preoccupation of the work. Rather than race being the primary lens through which the work should be viewed, racism was discussed as a prevailing reality of our context in the church and wider society, but our focus would be the empowerment of black churches to engage with each other and with white mainstream churches; and to focus on provision of resources by and about black churches. Viewed in this way, the work I would lead would engage in the struggle for justice but it would do so less by special pleading and more by black assertion. I have to admit to a fair amount of 'leading the witness' during the day.

We decided that that as black Christians we were not fighting to get a seat at the table of God, we were already there by God's grace and favour and we needed to assertively participate. And the gathering gave me a to-do list that included; building appropriate networks, including African, Caribbean and Asian, training and accreditation, accountability and transparency, youth, developing a new generation of leaders, accessing information and sharing resources, finding one political voice, celebrating together. It was agreed to call the new enterprise Minority Ethnic Christian Affairs (MECA). We found a Chairman too for MECA, Bishop Simon Iheanacho of UK World Evangelism Trust - yet again an organisation that was not a member of Churches Together. I wrote a strategic document and set to work as Secretary of MECA.

As I previously mentioned, I was not happy that of the churches that were members of Churches Together, several of the larger more notable ones were not. Alongside developing strategies to deliver what I had been mandated to do, supported by a Reference Group drawn from member and non-member black churches, I began a programme of visiting with the national heads of these larger black churches. I had a bit of a head start; being a bishop in one of them meant that I was known by the national leaders I was encouraging into Churches Together membership. Evidently, my being a member of staff of Churches Together provided some assurance for these theologically conservative churches – although they all knew I was not nearly as theologically conservative as many of them were. That didn't really matter because I did not wear my neo-liberalism on my sleeve and though we may have had some differences of emphasis, I was one of them.

In addition to my own assumptions, it was soon confirmed why these leaders had not seriously considered joining the Churches Together ecumenical instruments; they were thought to be too doctrinally, theologically, morally and ethically liberal; they were not concerned with the issues black communities faced; they did not take black faith seriously as evidenced by their willingness to allow the smaller black churches to speak on behalf of the black churches though self-evidently the larger more influential ones were outside the ecumenical room.

There was also high level of suspicion of white leadership. This became evident in that although theologically better disposed to the Evangelical Alliance and although most were members, some did not feel at home there either; the difference for us was that they joined the Evangelical Alliance albeit with low levels of involvement. This did not change significantly even when years later the Evangelical Alliance appointed a black General Director, Rev'd Joel Edwards. I had myself served as a Council member of the Alliance without feeling that I managed to offer much more than decorative value – another black face around the table. I had much better feeling of making meaningful contributions serving on other committees of the Evangelical Alliance.

I had some trump cards to play in my recruitment drive to strengthen the authenticity of the black presence within Churches Together. I realised that it was not the policy of the ecumenical instruments to seek to recruit members; it was not an evangelical organisation in that way. It had started with the mainstream or historic churches in membership in 1990, determined to behave differently from the old British Council of Churches it replaced, allowing churches to act rather than acting on their behalf. This non-evangelical stance meant that churches that wished to join would have to make the approach. I knew instinctively however that would not work for the churches I wanted to join Churches Together.

There needed to be an intentional effort to invite or encourage those churches to make an approach enquiring about membership. Then on the question of the liberal space that Churches Together was thought to represent, my line was to suggest that if the mainline churches were in error, it was not the place of their black brothers and sisters to ignore them since the bible implores; 'We who are strong ought to bear with the failings of the weak and not to please ourselves' (Rom 15.1 NIV). It was a near irresistible argument until one reminded me that the bible also says, 'Come out from them and be separate, says the Lord. Touch no unclean thing, and I will receive you (2 Cor 6.17). We called it a 1:1 draw.

There were other good reasons why these churches should consider becoming members of Churches Together such as the leaders knew well that some of the children in local churches had either been denied or had a difficult time getting into

Church of England schools that mandated church membership in Churches Together of the family's church. And they knew of the difficulties some of their ministers had finding jobs as chaplains in hospitals and prisons because of similar membership requirements of the churches they belonged to. My favourite card was a much more subtle one that played on the egos of some. My rhetorical question was, where else do you think you will get to share a table with the national leaders of Britain's churches, including the Archbishop of Canterbury and the Catholic Archbishop?'

Then more positively and assertively I would inevitably add, 'I would like to see you around that national church leaders table'. I knew they wanted to be there too! With all of these individual conversations came a free lunch as these men's sense of hospitality always meant that as I was visiting on their turf, they would feed me. This was not turning out to be a bad job after all. And slowly but surely the membership applications started to come in followed by the slow and deliberate process of discernment by member churches of Churches Together when an application for membership was received.

Today, as I write, approximately 40% of Churches Together's membership come from black and/or Pentecostal and Charismatic churches and agencies. I am not responsible for all of them joining but the momentum created in the early 2000s and the continued presence of a Pentecostal Bishop in the national ecumenical organisation has had some effect, I think.

To describe all the things I, with others, have accomplished from 2002/3 to today would result in a book much bigger than the one I propose here. But a saunter through some headlines will have to suffice as explanation of how the work I lead has become probably the most recognisable black Church and Pentecostal ecumenical reference point in Britain.

Well, sometimes I am reminded that among other drivers, the perceived fragmentation of the black Church context in Britain was a key motivator for seeking opportunity to move away from narrow deformational life and ministry and move into ecumenism. I saw it as a ministry of reconciliation (cf 2

Cor 5.18). As I discovered in Birmingham, before black church leaders were ready for black/white relationship there needed to be a process of black/black consolidation and affirmation.

Now on a national level the lack of acquaintance between fellow black leaders appeared to be stark. It was not hostility that existed between them, though there may have been some old animosities, but mainly it seemed estrangement was the result of leaders focussing on the work they were doing in a denominationally blinkered way that cried out for ecumenical intervention. These leaders just didn't seem to meet much. Maybe the most yawning gap was that between African and Caribbean heritage leaders. However, once I began to visit and move amongst these black national leaders I discovered that this alienation really was more a matter of perception than actuality. These leaders knew each other very well in pockets and small circles. Some of them had long historical ties of belongings and separations that meant they kept in touch and sometimes supported each other below the radar out of sight of their followers and the wider public.

The public face of separation and division belied ongoing undercover relationships. I understood part of my role as being to help this to appear above the radar. Quite often it was a case of blind man's bluff because the memberships of these churches cross related especially so among the young who had little regard for denominational boundaries and ignored them for the membership of their choirs, bands and much beside.

One earlier example of my attempt to network these leaders and their churches came when Bethel United Church of Jesus Christ under the leadership of Bishop Sydney Dunn bought a piece of land in West Bromwich in the Midlands. Having learned of their intention to build a convention centre, I made a daring attempt to turn the project into a joint one involving the New Testament Church of God, Church of God of Prophecy and Bethel.

In a meeting with Bishop Dunn I asked if he had thought of developing the site in such a tripartite partnership and instead of building a three thousand seater, build a five thousand one. I developed a picture of the economy of scale that could be achieved if instead of going it alone he had the other two significant national black Church on board as partners.

I imagined with the land situated close to the M5 motorway junction, hoteliers and other business partners may have emerged, and sourcing funding for a partnership was much more likely than for a denomination going alone. Bishop Dunn warmed to the idea and I convened three meetings of these churches' national leadership teams. This was the first time that the three national heads had met and we developed a real head of steam, resourced by a scoping paper I wrote. Sadly, after the third meeting it became clear that for a mix of ecclesial and financial reasons the joint venture was not going ahead.

Bishop Dunn's Bethel is an Oneness Pentecostal church while the other two are Trinitarian Pentecostal churches and this distinction was highlighted by some; while financially, the three were not aligned, with one being critically strapped for cash. I was sorely disappointed to see Bethel revert to its original plan to build a three thousand seater auditorium and to manage the process solo.

A second example was when the Church of God of Prophecy and the New Testament Church of God agreed to sign a strategic working together Memorandum of Understanding. I was asked to be the moderator of the signing service to mark the development; I called it playing the midwife. This bi-lateral understanding was an ecumenist delight and warm words were spoken; but after the signing little real integration or collaboration occurred, for various reasons again including economics.

But the main way in which I found success in developing black/black church and individual relations has been through seminars targeted at the black church constituency for leaders or leaders' representatives. By bringing leaders into the same room to hear about and discuss issues relevant to them, such as black underachievement in education, overrepresentation of black people in prisons and the wider Criminal Justice System, child abuse linked to witchcraft, difficulties with planning departments over change of use for places of worship, and youth concerns such as gangs, drugs, guns and knife; black deaths in police custody; mental health and many other issues, black church leaders have seen more of one another and have become more acquainted.

These conversations have helped to normalise many relations between leaders of Trinitarian Pentecostals and Oneness Pentecostals, between denominations like the Seventh Day Adventists and Pentecostals, between Caribbean and African churches, and between euro-centric African Pentecostals and African-centric often white-garmented African churches. I have been fascinated by these differences between churches and my mission was not to blend or merge them, it had been to bring people into conversation and relationship as a mark of the oneness I believe all Christians share.

I could not claim that as a result of these conversations a state of religious chumminess existed between the various Christian traditions black people follow, or that the relations built between those leaders who participated seamlessly trickled down to grassroots. However, my experience was that grassroots generally discovered good relationships across denominational and national lines long before their leaders did; so it was the leaders who played catch-up; though their leadership in relational areas, when known about, provided a kind of green light, a legitimising of what may have been normative among their members.

I have also worked at black church/white church relationships from my position in Churches Together. This has taken and continues to take many forms from exemplar to apologist, from advocate to educator. At times, I am proxy for 'the black church' in situations where there is no other black church person in the room and yet the position of the black church needed and was expected to be represented. I was often struck by the sheer patronising arrogance of some, not all, white religious leaders whose assumptions that regulated their relationships with black churches and their leaders seemed to regard black churches as bastardised versions of the Christian church, cults at best; people that led inadequate existences; needing therefore to be rescued and brought into fellowship with the authentic version of the Christian faith.

I have had to fight a rear guard battle in print and in vocalising that black churches lived full existences; they did not shrivel in cold extremities of the kingdom of God waiting to be rescued by white knights in shining armour. Some were indeed small and vulnerable, some lacked training, some lacked confidence to participate in wider relations; but none of them saw themselves as inferior forms of Christianity compared to Catholics, Anglicans, et al. I once made a presentation to the executives of a white-majority council explaining the contours of the Black Church Movement in Britain: its origins, life and future. At the conclusion of my talk and on the way out to go to lunch one executive said, 'I wouldn't describe it as a Damascus Road experience, but I certainly had a light bulb moment during your talk.'

It was fair to say that even amongst the more enlightened and well-disposed white leaders in Britain's churches, ignorance has prevailed. Sometimes this came across, in clumsy words and awkward deeds, as racism; but in my experience apart from the residual entrenched racism that runs through euro-centric thought like a blackpool rock, what was on show was often the product of ignorance of some white people who had never encountered or have had insufficient exposure to the black experience of faith.

Some white leaders were, I found, misled by the manner of life of some black Christians in mainstream churches who adopted an aloofness towards their fellow black Christians from the black churches thereby feeding the belief that Euro-Christianity was a higher life form. It has been my pleasure and duty to disabuse some of my white Christian brothers and sisters of these false notions of superiority. Having said what I did about some of my white brothers and sisters in leadership, it should not go unsaid that there have been significant departures from the well-meaning, liberal yet patroniser way.

Ever since my days as Director of the Centre for Black and White Christian Partnership I have been inundated with invitations to speak, lecture, preach or simply be present in white settings by people who seem keen to hear from and about the black Church constituency. Over these years, I have travelled the length and breadth of these British Isles, in secular and religious settings. I would like to think that some of the invitations have come because of me and what I as a person had to offer, not just because I was an expert on black Churches. I am unlikely to forget the experience of travelling from home in Birmingham to St Andrews University, Scotland that necessitated overnight travel and stay, to preach in a Sunday morning Church service in the chapel – for a maximum of ten minutes!

When it came to resources for and about the black Churches in Britain, you could say I was precisely that. This is in no way to imply that I was the only one, far from it. There had been in fact a growing number of black Church specialists emerging all the time and I welcomed this. These were primarily research students, many of whom contacted me from time to time to 'pick your brain' as they sometimes put it and others taking an interest in intercultural ecumenism. I sometimes felt like an unpaid tutor, supervisor and mentor – but that may be the added value of becoming an elder statesman.

Then there were the resources of the first generation of black Church leaders, members and practitioners. A few churches had accepted the challenge of capturing the experiences of their pioneers before they passed on and had published their histories or in individual cases people had published biographies and autobiographies. For my part, I had been writing, editing and publishing since the 1980s when I first appeared as a writer in Exodus Magazine, edited by Andrea Encinas and published by entrepreneur, Movery Livingstone.

My church's national and international magazines, the Messenger of Truth and the White Wing Messenger respectively also gave me opportunities to write. I have gone on to write in National black newspapers like the Journal and the Voice; and other magazines and newspapers. All of the time I have been passionate to portray my Christian community as a people precious to me and having something worthwhile to contribute to the wider world.

At the height of the national crisis in youth gangs and related issues of the use of drugs, guns and knives during the 2000s, I tried hard to fight the stigma that this was an exclusively black problem. One only needed to remember that Stephen Lawrence's stabbing to death in April 1993 was in fact perpetrated by white youths upon an innocent black youth and his friend Dwayne Brooks. I sought resources to conduct research into what I have come to regard as an urban social phenomenon in a British urban context where black and white youths exist cheek by jowl in a state of social, economic and political alienation and poverty.

The resulting publication, 'Who is My Neighbour – a church response to social disorder linked to gangs, drugs guns and knives', was then shared with the churches as I took a roadshow across the country explaining the challenges and exploring what churches, black and white, could try to do about them. For some this further stigmatised the black churches but I believed it was better to provide some intelligence on this thorny issue on the basis it was better to be criticised for getting involved with a challenge and taking some flack than the converse. I engaged in a number of such challenges over the years seeking to make resources available to assist the churches; such as serving on the Steering Group of the government's task force and subsequent National Action Plan to tackle child abuse linked to witchcraft.

I served also as a member of a group of advisors to the Labour Government on a programme titled 'REACH - an independent report to Government on raising the aspirations and attainment of black boys and young black men'. Over those years, several pieces of information were developed and shared within and beyond, by and about the black church and wider community; and I have been blessed to contribute in some way.

Has it all helped? Who knows! I honestly believe the church and the wider world would be the worst for not having had these and other interventions even though the impact of the 'silver bullet' is never felt, because it does not exist. What exists is painfully slow and deliberate action that we hope makes, however small, a contribution to improving the communities we live in.

In supporting the work of black churches in Britain through my job at Churches Together the mundane can get a little exotic at times. Politicians, Government ministers and departments,

High Commissions and other high-level secular and religious agencies, including the very occasional contact with royalty, seek my perspective on how best to relate to a constituency they tend to not know enough about. While few of the main personalities would know me personally, they often utilise the product and expertise of my office.

I am in no doubt that mine is not the only agency that receives such approaches, but there is something about being situated within the national ecumenical instrument to which the significant religious institutions, including the State Church, belong. It is something akin to being within the BBC among broadcasters; you are not the only one, or the most exciting, but people think of you as reliable and trustworthy. I hope the advice and support I give matches their expectations, but I can never really know.

I rest peacefully after every day's work in the knowledge I always give my best in my determination to see the black church in Britain that has nurtured me put its best foot forward internally and externally. Of course it is not all down to me, and there are aspects of the black church that do not match my expectations, but life is what it is and I try to work with what is to make it what I would like it to be – however long that may take.

I mentioned above that after years of working full-time, including my six years as Director of the Centre for Black and White Christian Partnership (1996-2002), since taking up my ecumenical role with Churches Together in 2002 I became a part-time employee. Once it became clear that a return to pastoral work in the Church of God of Prophecy was not likely as we had grown apart and those in authority seemed to have no appetite to consider such a prospect; and as I knew that I could not be a loyal gatekeeper to denominational creeds and customs I no longer stood by, I began to explore how to create additional income.

It was not a strain. On the one hand, there was a steady stream of invites to preach, speak, lecture; not sufficient to live on, but adequate as a supplement. On the other hand, flowing from the community involvement that had become part and parcel of my public ministry, once I was more available I found my gifts and talents in demand. Four pieces of paid work, alongside a host of voluntary ones, buttressed my work at Churches Together until 2014 when my ecumenical post became full-time. But before mentioning these important pieces of work, I need to locate them within a crucial piece of socio-spiritual intervention that developed in Birmingham from around 1997 – the previously mentioned Council of Black Led Churches (CBLC).

In a wholly voluntary capacity, I served CBLC in a six year period as vice-chair, then a further six years as chair, between 1997 and 2009. During this time, the CBLC was viewed in the press as the 'go to' black-led ecumenical agency on matters relating to the black community and black faith. We were invited to intervene in numerous strategies and situations. Once we were called upon to provide a Chair for a struggling black-led government sponsored education and employment project: The Birmingham Partnership for Change; I became the Chair.

As leaders, Bishop Derek Webley and I were often in the press commenting on various developments especially linked to the phenomenon of gangs. But this reputation was earned by the serious work we did on the ground among the churches and in the community. We marched, we lobbied, we held celebrations, we counselled, we served on committees and boards, we collaborated and we led.

A highlight of my time as Chair of CBLC was the 2007 national bicentenary commemoration of the Parliamentary Act of 1807 to abolish the Atlantic Slave Trade. That year I chaired Birmingham City Council's response called 'Breaking the Chains', and led CBLC's response the highlight of which was a service at the Bethel Convention Centre, West Bromwich that attracted some three thousand people, by far the largest gathering anywhere in the country that year to mark the event.

I reckon I read and learned more in that one year about chattel slavery and the rigours of that inhumane industry in human misery as told by the narratives of the enslaved than I had ever done. It was a struggle to remain positive about white people that year having repeatedly been reminded of some of the despicable acts that were committed by white Europeans against my African ancestors. And to cap it all, to learn that when slavery finally ended in the British West Indies in 1834, the slave owners were compensated to the tune of £20 million for loss of property, whilst the enslaved were simple turned off the estates to fend for themselves in the bush.

Much of the wealth of Europe, the poverty of the former enslaved and their colonies, and therefore the current inequalities are rooted in that barbarous slave industry. It remains my view that Europe must pay reparations, right their wrong, do the Zacchaeus act of restitution (Luke 19.8) which requires more than an apology in words alone.

Some of the early targets of CBLC were education, health and the police. We tended to request, it may have seemed like 'demand', meetings with heads of services from the City Council to Police Chief to Health Authority chief. We were rarely if ever refused which proved the power of organising. I was very keen to see the black Church leaders being respected and consulted on the issues that affected our community and a rejuvenated CBLC since 1997 became the catalyst for being accorded this respect.

I took a close interest in education and health. We rewarded high achievement in education at CBLC's annual awards ceremony, we conducted education seminars, health seminars and spent many hours with education and health specialists and bureaucrats challenging norms and making suggestions. My first part-time job in health came about when the CEO of the Birmingham Health Authority suggested I accept a role on the Management Committee of a Primary Care Group (PCG).

'But I know nothing about health', I protested.

'You'll pick it up as you go along', said Brian Stouten.

I think this was his way of shutting me up and getting a bit of his own back for the angst I and CBLC had been giving him.

After a few months of serving on this health committee, the government's reform of the National Health Service resulted in the creation and transfer of duties to Primary Care Trusts (PCTs). The Non-Executive Directors (NEDs) of the old NHS bodies were required to all step down and re-apply for any posts in the new structure. I was pressed to apply to become Chair of one of the four PCTs to cover the city of Birmingham.

With continued reservation about my lack of health service knowledge, but constantly being encouraged to stay around to dispense my impartial wisdom, leaving the health judgement to the professionals, I applied to be Chair of the huge £500 million health trust and was duly appointed. Was this really happening? Yes, it was and now I had the task of choosing my Chief Executive Officer. My choice was an inspired one, I still feel, the bright and energetic Sophia Christie who has gone on to make quite a name for herself. We got on very well and were well served by excellent staff.

I led on the appointment of senior staff too and was deeply disappointed that on no occasion was I able to appoint a black person to a Director's post. There were scarcely any who applied and the few that did, fell short, usually due to lack of preparation or familiarity with pitching for these big jobs. The 'pastor' in me meant I had a steady stream of people wanting to see me for all sorts much of which were not in the gift of the Chair, but people felt better it seems after having had a chat with the seemingly all powerful chairman. I did not feel powerful. In fact, most of the time I felt out of my depth, certainly on health matters which were difficult to separate from being chair of a health trust! This was a proper half-time job alongside my work with Churches Together, and I was kept very busy indeed.

As Chairman, I took it upon myself to visit all the medical practices in my Trust's area of Birmingham. It took a while, but my excellent PA arranged it all and I was so glad I did it; and so were the GPs who generally felt managers had too much power and were always pleased to explain to the Chair how the Health Service should really be run – by doctors, of course. On one memorable visit to a practice, I had a fruitful meeting with the practice partners and was on my way out. As I reached near the exit door one of the practice doctors broke ranks with the others and quietly asked if they could see me for a minute. Once in their room the doctor said to me, 'Bishop Aldred, tomorrow I am having an operation; please will you pray with me?'

'Of course', I said, held their hands and prayed.

I was deeply moved. This was one of those poignant moments when Chairman and Bishop met in me.

Once when we interviewed for some sub-director management positions, I became increasingly irritated by the Eurocentric cultural limitations of the assessment processes that adversely affected the Panel's capacity to appoint non-white persons. I paused the process, tweaked the requirements in ways that valued also non-European cultural mores which allowed us to appoint at least one person that day who was from an ethnic minority background. I was pleased with myself. There were things that really troubles me in the NHS. The arbitrary nature of some appointments and the favouritism that accompanied some of that. I was baffled by the waste of money on continuous 'organisational change'. It felt like the NHS was in a constant state of flux and change, made worse by making available little pots of money at short notice that required staff to spend hours preparing to submit bids to meet impossible deadlines.

Although my CEO and the Executive Directors were doing well – we balanced our books, engaged effectively with our public, and had efficiently chaired public meetings - I continued to feel that I was not in the most appropriate place as Chair of a PCT. And as happens when there are doubts, metaphorical water finds metaphorical cracks. Out of the blue, whilst at home one evening with an old friend standing in the doorway to my study as I tapped away on my word processor, my telephone rang.

It was Pastor Clifford Fryer from the Cannon Street Memorial Baptist Church in Handsworth, Birmingham. I knew him a little having taken students to visit his church when I was Director of the Centre for Black and White Christian Partnership. On one of those visits, I had thought out loud about how much I loved the feel of the church and would love to pastor here one day. It was a sigh, a throwaway remark. However, in this telephone call Clifford reminded me of my comments which he had heard, stored and now acted upon. The church had been on the lookout for a senior black pastor and Clifford brought to the attention of the deacons what he had heard me say some time ago. He sought and got permission to contact me to check my interest in the position of becoming an associate pastor with an eye on his own retirement – which I interpreted as an invitation to become senior pastor after his departure. It was to prove more complex than that.

After quite a bit of activity, a lengthy period of discernment and the kind of conversations you have when you cross denominational lines, I decided to accept their call to join the pastoral team at Cannon Street Memorial Baptist Church. I dropped the bombshell at the Primary Care Trust one morning in our weekly Executive Team meeting. My CEO was shocked and quite emotional. I had not expected that reaction. Sophia really didn't get it; why was I leaving such a successful team? She eventually composed herself and said, 'I suppose I can't compete with God.' To her credit and my delight Sophia attended my induction when it came and we continued to keep in touch for years after I had left the trust.

It was a much more painful break than I had expected to leave the Primary Care Trust. I felt it was the right decision because I was returning, albeit in a part-time capacity, to my main vocation as a pastor alongside my ecumenical work with Churches Together. The Health Service was to have a very long tail. The people who had come to know me kept finding ways to shoehorn me into things. Again encouraged, I applied for and became a Board Member of the Birmingham and Solihull Mental Health Trust, a remunerated position; before stepping down from that and offering myself as an unpaid Governor of the same trust.

I was duly elected and served as Governor until 2010. After my successor as Chair of the Primary Care Trust was appointed, businessman Paul Sabapathy, he being also Lord Lieutenant, invited me to become one of his Deputy Lieutenants (DL). I thought long and hard about this and much to his disappointment, said no. I was not comfortable with the prospect of accompanying visiting royalty and discovered in myself strains not of anti-royalty, but of republicanism. In similar vein I find myself thinking hard what I would do were I ever to be offered a Queen's honour that was linked to empire like 'Member of the British Empire (MBE).

I am not sure I could accept that either. The British Empire does not exist anymore anyway so why base national honours on a lost entity which many former colonised peoples have mixed feelings at best and contempt for at worst? I have not had to make that decision as yet but would struggle to say yes, notwithstanding my family telling me I would have to accept. Maybe we shall find out one day, who knows? Every now and then I run into someone from my days involved with the Health Service and it's always with good memories that people seem to recall my time as Chairman, committee and board member, and Governor. I recall undergoing a 360 degrees assessment programme during my time as Chair, to be told by the assessor that looking at the scores and comments from those who contributed to my assessment, our meeting was going to be a counsel of perfection. I was clearly highly thought of, even as I was uncomfortable in the role.

I have grown up a Pentecostal and although since the start of my pastoral ministry I have sought ecumenical relationships outside my tradition, I had only ever experienced pastoral appointment within my tradition. So the process of the 'call' to pastoral ministry in a Baptist church was destined to prove challenging. Baptists are congregational; which means unlike the Church of God of Prophecy that is run from the centre with pastoral appointments made by the National Overseer and/or District Overseer with minimal to no local church input; each local Baptist Church selects its own pastor with minimal involvement from the centre.

Notwithstanding that the initial approach to me was made by the 'senior' pastor on behalf of the deacons, there was still to follow a pretty rigorous process of examination and discernment by the local church lead by the board of twelve deacons. I 'preached with a view' twice, and had two 'interview' meetings with the deacons, in addition to liaisons with the national and regional Baptist Associations which, although not determinative in the appointment, had inputs, as did the existing pastor and trainee pastor. Because I was not an ordained Baptist Minister, the Baptist Union of Great Britain had to consider the appropriateness or legitimacy of my existing ordination in the Church of God of Prophecy.

By this time, I was a bishop in the Church of God of Prophecy, had a Master's degree in theology and was on the verge of completing my PhD. Not to mention my years of pastoral and oversight ministry and much management and chairman's experience. They approved me for ministry in the Baptist Church without equivocation. I needed to clear the matter of pastoring in a different denomination with my own church hierarchy too. This was granted – a little too willingly I felt.

For my part, I made it clear to the Baptist Church that I would remain in my half time post as an ecumenist with Churches Together in England – which considering the paltry full-time pay on offer was just as well - and that I would not resign from being a bishop in the Church of God of Prophecy. Cannon Street Baptist Church made some concessions in allowing me to be paid their full-time salary although I would officially work half-time and I held dual membership and ministry credentials in both churches. Although I had made a decision to become a pastor in a Baptist Church I had not made a decision to leave the the Church of God of Prophecy.

In September 2003, I began my tenure as Associate Pastor. The team was Rev'd Clifford Fryer, a longstanding (white) minister with eighteen months to go to retirement, home-grown trainee minister, Bryan Scott and I, a senior black Pentecostal Bishop, brought in, so it appeared and so I understood it, to take over as senior pastor when Clifford retired. I figured I had eighteen months to learn how to be a Baptist.

At my induction service, I spoke about a plane taking off and how in order to get to one's destination there would be turbulence en route, indeed turbulence was a kind of necessary companion on a flight going somewhere. I had as main speaker my good friend Rev'd Joel Edwards, General Director of the Evangelical Alliance who used the term 'Bapticostal' to describe my new post. And one of my favourite singers, Carla Hales, sang beautifully.

The place was rammed and the atmosphere of optimism was palpable. God had brought us together in a cross-denominational partnership that felt right. I had, however, taken the precaution that I wanted a review after twelve months so we didn't get locked into something that was not working; even so in my heart I hoped that at fifty I would see out my working pastoral life at this church.

Given where I was theologically, the Baptist church actually suited me more than my own Pentecostal denomination; a fact that was to prove disappointing for those who were frustrated Pentecostals in the Baptist church gladdened by news that a Pentecostal pastor was joining the team. Some found me to be less Pentecostal than they had hoped.

I realised during the first year that this was not going well. For various reasons I became aware that whilst the overwhelming majority of the congregation were having the time of their lives, proud to have a black pastor who as some put it, was an articulate, intelligent, educated and inspirational black preacher and pastor; there definitely was a vociferous minority for whom I was not what they had bargained for. A dream come true for some was a nightmare for others.

The three pastors, of which I was one, worked quite well for the most part, with each having responsibility for a third of the twelve deacons in the diaconate and the ministries under them. We met weekly to discuss and plan. I took to my brief with gusto and initiated a string of initiatives bringing in volunteers to contribute, several of whom said they had not before been part of the 'clique' that ran the church.

I launched a monthly glossy magazine, a weekly newsletter, rebranded the church literature such as letterheads projecting a corporate image under the acronym CSMBC. I started a creative theological discussion group for the intelligent 'seeker' and preached my heart out regularly on Sundays as we three pastors took turns to preach Sunday mornings and evenings. Along with visiting and caring for an aging church with a busy funeral diary, we found the church growing from the various streams that flowed into the river that was the rebirthed CSMBC. However, as I have hinted not everyone was pleased with me or with some of the people I was using to get the work done – former outsiders turned active insiders.

As well as we were doing, I was clear that if CSMBC were to move forward doing the kinds of things I believed it could do then it needed a senior pastor with authority and currently the three pastors were equal in authority – a novel idea in principle but hugely problematic in practice.

There were too many times for my liking when there needed to be one decision-maker, a person with whom the buck stopped, when we were an equal threesome in authority with irreconcilable differences of opinions. The situation often, in my view, cried out for a senior pastor. It was clear to me that at least some of the deacons knew that too; and that tough decisions needed to be made to rid the church of some of the sacred cows of traditions and customary behaviours, to include some of the excluded and exclude some of the included: this was not going to be best done by committee.

I was more than willing to be that senior pastor, indeed I went to CSMBC with the understanding that after eighteen months that would happen. When within my first year it began to look like I would be that person because I was already acting more decisively than my colleagues, those who had other ideas about whether and who a senior pastor should be began to bare their dissenting teeth. It was not pretty.

The anniversary review I had asked for was conducted and it seemed to me I did not have the support of the whole diaconate so I decided that I had to consider my position. I am not a fan of muddled leadership, preferring to side with leadership guru John Maxwell that everything stands or falls on leadership; and I am a believer in the biblical principle that 'if the trumpet does not sound a clear call, who will get ready for battle? (1 Cor 14.8). The membership of CSMBC were shocked when it became clear I was planning to leave after just over one year.

There were recriminations, skulduggery, and quite some unpleasantness; but I decided that what had emerged was not what I had anticipated and therefore it was best for me to move on, regrettably. I gave a lengthy notice and after just over two years at CSMBC, I left. To be perfectly honest, I did not find it hard to leave once I had decided that was the right thing to do, however it may have appeared to others.

Continuing my part-time work as an ecumenist with Churches Together in England, I soon accepted to head up a project with Birmingham City Council looking at black school exclusions. I was astonished at the amount of children who were not attending school because they had been excluded, some officially, others unofficially – many for what appeared to be spurious or at best challengeable reasons and often the parents learned after the event by receiving a telephone call to collect their child.

With money from Birmingham City Council, I and some key educationalists in Birmingham, among them Rosemary Campbell Stephens and Kembi Clarke, under Partnership for Achievement (PfA), worked to bridge a gap of understanding between school and home, parent and teacher in the interest of the education of the child. PfA published and disseminated a parent's guide to exclusion that the local Authority Education Department talked about adopting for city-wide distribution through schools; I don't think that ever happened.

We conducted a two-year campaign to raise awareness of the disproportionately high rate of the exclusions of black pupils and the low rate of black employment. One particular battle I led in the employment sector was to argue with big employers, like the banks, that they could not look for employees from the black community in an urban area like Birmingham and yet insist they will not employ anyone with a 'record'. 'You cannot be serious' I said in one meeting. My point was that so many people in urban areas like Birmingham, struggling to survive, had County Court Judgements (CCJs) often for petty crimes or for such as TV Licence non-payment that to have such a rule became discriminatory and unhelpful. They got the point and moderated their policy.

A combination of the kind of work I was now doing at Partnership for Achievement and as the voluntary Chair of the Council of Black Led Churches led to the offer from one of the leaders of Birmingham City Council for me to become an Ambassador for the African and Caribbean community in Birmingham, appointed by the City. My community was certainly in need of a boost and an advocate, so I thought long and hard about this, consulted widely, but decided against it. The politicians were disappointed but rather like when I was invited to become Deputy Lieutenant (DL), I felt this would take me in an area of quasi politics I did not want to go. In the case of the DL, it did not fit with my socio-political views, and now becoming a politically appointed Ambassador I felt would make me too much the politician and bring my Christian Minister, ecumenical and other roles into question as to political motivation for what I did and argued for.

I had already got into trouble once when during a challenging moment with Birmingham gangs I was interviewed on television, with unknown to me, a title under my name that read, 'Community Leader'. Well, certain quarters of the community were, I was told, up in arms. Who made me a community leader, some wanted to know. In Jamaica they say you must 'take sleep mark death' and I knew that if I wanted to 'represent' I needed to run for elected office, something I did not want to do, preferring to remain a-political. By remaining so, some precious opportunities presented themselves; like when, with a Sikh leader, I visited the grieving parents of a Muslim youth who had died in one of the disturbances in Birmingham. It was a truly moving experience of interfaith, non-politically aligned compassionate action.

PfA closed after its two year scheduled life having done some significant cajoling, prompting and agitating. Leaders in the city of Birmingham were very cooperative with us trying to raise the bar in education and employment. I discovered that they often simply did not know what to do and I, with others, tried to assist from within the community. Although this and other community work was rewarding, I found that no matter how hard I worked, how exhausted I became, how much I felt I had achieved, it was never enough. The problem whether in education or employment was always bigger than me. I resolved to keep trying from whichever vantage point I found myself.

I tend not to wear my faith on my sleeve, but my life is rooted deeply in a belief that God is in control of my life and destiny and that I exist to self-fulfil and to help others do the same because every person is made in the image and likeness of God, having a purpose to fulfil. Within this cosmology, I have found doors opening as soon as others closed. So it was that a significant development emerged when I least expected and was not looking for it, in the field of broadcasting.

Whilst a pastor at Cannon Street Memorial Baptist Church in early 2000s I visited the local black community radio station – the only licenced one – in the city of Birmingham. I merely wanted to familiarise myself with the people behind it and offer my moral support. I met Martin Blissett, the manager of the Afro Caribbean Millennium Centre (ACMC), the parent body of New Style Radio. For most of the time Martin doubled up as station manager. After showing me around, he told me he had looked forward to my visit because he had a proposal to put to me. He had heard and seen me in the media and liked what he heard and saw, so wondered if I would consider doing a Gospel Show on New Style Radio.

There were already some Gospel shows on New Style Radio, I reminded him. Martin was very clear that in addition to existing programmes he wanted something that raised the intellectual discourse about faith, not only play Gospel music. I had not presented a radio programme before and needed quite some time and some persuasion to say yes. For two years on a wholly voluntary basis I presented this Gospel music and talk show from 7.00 to 8.00AM on Sundays. It proved highly popular.

The station provided some coaching too which helped me enormously. I was reminded often though that this was a station that ran largely on volunteerism as things did not always run smoothly. Over the two years, there were the odd Sunday morning when I along with my producer could not gain access to the building to broadcast, and occasions when I would do a pre-recorded show because I was away on the Sunday only to discover the broadcast never happened because someone overslept or some other reason. I decided to stop doing it.

With two years of live radio broadcasting under my belt, daringly, I emailed the Editor of my local BBC Radio Station, BBC WM, telling him of my media experience including in community radio and that should any broadcasting vacancy occur I would be interested. This was not done totally out of the blue because over the years I had featured in interviews quite often expressing my opinion on a range of topics, particularly matters to do with African and Caribbean faith, culture and politics. The Editor was well aware of me.

There also was an African and Caribbean programme on the station that I had listened and contributed to and sometimes felt I could present should the opportunity present itself. Well, to my great surprise and pleasure I arrived in my office one late afternoon after a long day on Churches Together business in London to find an email from the BBC Editor, inviting me to come in and see him. The presenter at the time, had tendered her resignation and the editor wanted to offer me the job of presenting the two hour live show – and for pay. Wow!

There was a little matter of doing a few pre-start trials with the Deputy Editor. These did not go well, and it is fair to say if I was being considered on the strength of my trial runs in the company of the Deputy Editor, I would not have been offered the job. I was abysmal. Trouble was I had done two years of highly scripted shows and was being asked to adlib in the BBC trial runs. Once I got some scripts, I was OK and things improved ahead of my start date in September 2007. I started to great razzmatazz.

A bishop was joining a local radio station presenting a non-religious programme. At the time of writing I am in my eighth year, now co-presenting the show called, 'Chatback' with Nikki Tapper. I had no idea I would last this long.

My local live show is part of a wider involvement with the BBC and other broadcasters and the press. I find myself fairly regularly interviewed and quoted in the black press, less so in mainstream press. But I have made it onto Newsnight (including the special treatment of having a chauffeur-driven BBC car collect and deliver me home) and a few other television programmes; and I have turned down a few too when I did not think they were appropriate for me.

I have enjoyed lengthy runs on BBC Radio 2's Pause for Thought, and BBC Radio 4's Prayer for the Day. Also on Radio 4, I have preached in the Sunday Service a few times, I have been on the Moral Maze, given a Lent Talk, All Things Considered and Beyond Belief. I really enjoyed doing 'All things considered' on BBC Radio Wales. And Premier Christian Radio has me as one of their regular 'go to' person on varying religious matters. All this and more have put an enormous strain on balancing a broadcasting career alongside a national ecumenical Christian ministry; and I have landed in trouble more than once.

The BBC in particular insists that I remember that I am a journalist and must never compromise their or my impartiality by my public pronouncements on controversial matters. I may be required to interview on my radio programme, for example, someone who may feel my declared position on a matter means they cannot guarantee fair treatment if being interviewed by me. I have learned to be diplomatic and qualified in what I say in public and overall I would say I have got the balance about right; but this has been at the expense of my being silent on some matters I would dearly love to pronounce on. Everything has its price and I love the facility to broadcast and explore issues relevant to faith and the black community.

It would be remiss of me to leave the topic of broadcasting and in particular the BBC without making a few observations. There have been a longstanding criticism of British mainstream media concerning its lack of diversity, of which the paucity of people of African and Caribbean heritage behind and in front of cameras, mics or national newspapers has led, it is argued, to ambitious black journalists and actors moving across the pond to the United States.

One only needs follow the press to realise that black people in the US do not have things all their own favourable way. However, it is clear that probably due to scale – African Americans total circa 45 million or 15% of the US population compared with African and Caribbean at 1 million and 2% of the British population - there are more opportunities in the US than in the UK. Notwithstanding the smaller numbers in Britain it can feel mighty alienating when one watches television, listen to radio read newspapers and magazines and scarcely see anyone looking like you.

I once encouraged a young man to tune in to my radio programme. He asked, 'which station?' 'BBC WM', I said. 'Oh, you mean the white people station?' he replied. And it does seem odd that in a city like Birmingham where I live and where the percentage of black and ethnic minorities is higher than the national average that a radio station like BBC Radio WM, does not have a presenter profile during week-day day-time programming, that matches the ethnic profile of its constituency. Things are changing slowly, but the challenge of the press and media is to reflect, as much as possible, the profile of its listenership in its frontline and backroom staffing. And the BBC ought to be a leader in this or run the risk of being viewed as a 'white people station' by those who do not see or hear themselves reflected. If black and minority people are kept at bay, it begs the question, why? And the answer may, reluctantly, be institutionalised racism, i.e. unwitting, but clear exclusion of ethnic minorities.

Because my post in Churches Together since 2002/3 has been part-time, I have done a number of things alongside my ecumenical role. From Chair, board member and governor in the NHS, to Pastor; from Managing Director to committee and board member. On occasions I have had to cull board and committee memberships, with resignations and refusals to join, which I find difficult to do; but understanding the necessity to cut back if I want to retain my sanity and not suffer burnout.

It is impossible to give a blow by blow of the things that have attended my life and work. What has already been said is a selective autobiographical sketch of my life to date and I want to mention two other matters. First, that since the start of 2014, my Churches Together post became full-time, in recognition of the growing Pentecostalism and black Church presence within the membership of Churches Together - my portfolio over the past decade or so.

At Churches Together, the Black and White Christian Partnership gave way to Minority Ethnic Christian Affairs, which gave way to Pentecostal and Multicultural Relations. Associated with this work, I have been very pleased to be associated with the appointment of the first Pentecostal President in a presidium of six within Churches Together in England; which I hope and believe will help Pentecostalism take its rightful place of eminence alongside other Christian faith streams. My task now is to work with this president in furthering the PMR portfolio.

A second important recent development is the creation of the National Church Leaders Forum (NCLF) – a black Christian voice that was set up by a number of black church leaders and practitioners around 2011. I have been keen for the black church in Britain to have a clear voice that proceeds from a place of independent integrity. I worked with the leadership of NCLF to produce 'Political Mobilisation – a manifesto for change' as the black church's attempt to highlight the political priorities that emerge from the context of black life in Britain ahead of the 2015 General Elections. Campaigning organisation Operation Black Vote (OBV) suggests there were over one hundred and fifty marginal seats where the 'Black Vote' could be determinative.

Colleagues and I in NCLF were determined that the so-called sleeping giant would awaken for the 2015 elections and developed the manifesto to assist that process. If I am to have a legacy I would love it to include my contribution to making the black churches in Britain a greater political and spiritual force affecting the manner and quality of the country's life.

Another would be assisting in the improvement of relationship between mainstream and black and Pentecostal churches through the engagements I have tried to develop and foster. And I would like to think that through the quality and consistency of my life, through broadcasting, ecumenism, speaking and writing I have contributed to greater diversity, justice, empowerment and liberation for my own people of African descent and the wider community including the church.

As I bring the curtain down on this autobiography my mind turns to the future. At sixty-two, I have reached a ripe age considering when I was young I wondered if I would live long enough to get married. I would dearly love to continue working for Churches Together in England until I hit seventy – I enjoy what I do so much I can hardly countenance the idea of retiring and drawing a pension; so delaying it five years beyond the normal retirement age is a good compromise. Of course, I am aware that how much time I have ahead of me is in part down to me and so I try to lead a healthy lifestyle. If it were down to me, then I would live to at least one hundred years old.

To date, my family have been a dream. Three daughters and four grandchildren to usher me into old age and beyond. My wife of forty years in 2014 and I have been through thick and thin and have more than survived, we have prospered together. I believe we have set high standards for ourselves and a pattern for our children and theirs. We have steadfastly trusted in God the Creator and Sustainer of our lives. In education, my wife has studied successfully to master's degree level, I have achieved a PhD.

I believe beyond a shadow of doubt that our solid partnership has facilitated this and I for one am an unqualified advocate of marriage as a foundation of family life. Finally, I have developed and lived by a world view that understands God alone as sovereign. So the idea that anybody is innately superior to me is completely beyond acceptability.

All of us are created in the image and likeness of the Creator, full of potential awaiting nourishing and development. I thank God that I have had the benefit of selfless nurturing that has enabled me to have achieved all that I have from a humble beginning. My thanks to everyone who have helped me along the way. And when it is all over here, I look forward to being with the Creator in eternity, having lived my life the best I knew how. In the meantime, I have come a long way from Top Mountain, but I have not reached my destination as yet! Whilst serving as pastor in Oxford, one of my young members then, wrote this poem at an appreciation service:

We do not know what lies ahead,
We only see what's now;
And like a farmer sowing seeds,
We reap the fields and plough.

The work looks great, the labourers few,
But what we oft don't see;
Is that the Lord is working too,
And he will grow the seeds.

He made a way for us before,
He'll make a way again;
He'll sift the wheat and tares, and
Soon we'll see that all is grain.

One day we'll stand before the Lord,
We'll see the Holy One;
With joy we'll hear the Master's words,
'Well done, you good and faithful servant, well done'.

(Wendy Mendez, Oxford, August 1988)